FROM
DREAM
to DESTINY

FROM
DREAM
TO DESTINY

KEYS TO UNLOCKING YOUR FUTURE

CLINTON C. BAKER

DESTINY IMAGE™ EUROPE srl
Via Maiella, 1
66020 San Giovanni Teatino (Ch) - Italy

"Changing the world, one book at a time."

This book and all other Destiny Image™ Europe books are available at Christian bookstores and distributors worldwide.

To order products, or for any other correspondence:

DESTINY IMAGE™ EUROPE srl
Via Acquacorrente, 6
65123 - Pescara - Italy
Tel. +39 085 4716623 - Fax +39 085 9431270
E-mail: info@eurodestinyimage.com

Or reach us on the Internet: **www.eurodestinyimage.com**

ISBN: 978-88-89127-88-9
For Worldwide Distribution, Printed in the U.S.A.
1 2 3 4 5 6 7 8/13 12 11 10 09

DEDICATION

I dedicate this book to the late Charles R. Bray, my father. When this dream was being birthed, he went home to be with the Lord. I thank him for providing an atmosphere of faith and love growing up, which allowed me an opportunity to succeed in life. He represents the face of so many homes where a stepfather comes in and takes care of a displaced child because of love and not obligation. I am thankful to God for sending you to be my dad and friend when I was a broken child, caught in the grief of divorce. You are greatly missed, but your lessons of survival have prepared the way to help me realize kingdom dreams can be turned into reality.

ACKNOWLEDGMENTS

Trust in the Lord with all thine heart; and lean not unto thine own understanding. In all thy ways acknowledge Him, and He shall direct thy paths (Proverbs 3:5-6).

First of all I acknowledge God the Father, His Son Jesus, and the Holy Spirit—without the ministry of each I am completely inadequate to live or function in every day life.

I want to acknowledge my wife, Beverly Baker, who has stood with me through the ups and downs, the highs and lows—not just of this project but for the last 20 years. To my mother, Rosa Bray, who has been a champion in life—my first mentor, coach, and caregiver. Thanks for watching over me and believing in me. You trusted God to save my soul and fulfill the will of God in my life.

To my assistant, Sheryl Ballenger, who has been an encourager throughout this project and helped me to meet deadlines, sacrificing to see things through to completion. To Deacon Willie Ballenger, for taking care of the material matters so I can give myself to the Word of God and prayer.

To Michael and Arrie Fowler, for your self-sacrifice to help us until completion. To Arlinda and Tara Glenn, for your love, service, and support through the years. We consider your service to God and us invaluable.

To Terry and Yolanda Pettigrew, thanks for asking no questions when called upon. To Pam Lynch, my hat's off to you for helping, calling, and being to us whatever is necessary to see that we fulfill the will of God.

To Dr. Larry Keefauver, for your wisdom, instruction, and editing of this manuscript. Your gift to see this project completed will definitely be rewarded in this life and the one to come.

To Pietro Evangelista, the publisher of Destiny Image Europe, for hearing from God about this prophetic message that the Body of Christ so desperately needs. Also, to everyone in the Destiny Image family who has worked under God's anointing to see this dream turned into reality. Thank you.

To Pastor Mike Eubanks, you have been there to encourage and hold up my hands without receiving a pat on the back; God was watching. To Dr. Darryl Webb, for introducing me to Pietro Evangelista. To Douglas Mallory, for always coming on a moment's notice to get the job done and help meet deadlines. Finally, to the followers of Christ Fellowship Church, for your love and support.

These acknowledgments are given to all those who assisted me during the writing of this book. If there is anyone I have failed to mention, please charge it to my head and not my heart.

TABLE OF CONTENTS

Foreword 13

Preface 17

Introduction..................................19

Chapter 1   Delight in the Lord then Dream 23

Chapter 2   The Dream Is About God 35

Chapter 3   Enlarge the Place of Your Tent 49

Chapter 4   Divine Connections 65

Chapter 5   I Have a Kingdom Dream 79

Chapter 6   A Word About Pursuing the Heart
of God by Dr. Ron Kenoly 95

Chapter 7   A Progression of Divine Connections 105

Chapter 8   Kingdom Dream—The Next Step 121

Chapter 9   A Word on Divine Interventions
               by Shekhar Kallianpur 135

Chapter 10   Manifesting Your Kingdom Dream.................149

Conclusion   Dream Kingdom Dreams! 163

FOREWORD

We all have dreams. Some of our dreams are clear with specific details and we want to always remember them. They are dreams that inspire us and cause us to work harder and reach higher to make those dreams a reality.

When I was younger I remember singing a song called the "Impossible Dream," which was a hit song from *Man of La Mancha*, the highly successful movie and stage production. That song and musical caused many who saw it to take their dreams more seriously no matter how unlikely they seemed to be in reality.

Many times I have heard that old cliche, "Shoot for the stars—if you make it to the moon you will have gone where only a select few have gone." It is those who dream that change the world and shape the future.

Martin Luther King Jr. dreamed that someday America would be a nation where its citizens would be judged by the content of their character and not by the color of their skin.

President John F. Kennedy dreamed that America would be the first nation to send a man to the moon.

Nelson Mandela spent 27 years in prison dreaming that his people in South Africa would someday live in freedom.

In the year 1492, Columbus acted upon his dream that he could find India by sailing west across the Atlantic Ocean.

There are thousands of others throughout history who were not intimidated by the vastness of their dreams or the opposition they would face by declaring what they had seen in their dreams.

Other dreams are dreams that we choose to forget. They might frighten us and cause us to pray and rebuke the events that occurred in the dream. Most of us have had nightmares that we feel come straight from the enemy to distract us from something that God has called us to do. Those are not kingdom dreams.

Whenever God gives a mandate through dreams and visions, you can be sure that satan will try to cause us to abort that mandate. There are many Bible stories of men who had dreams that came from God, and satan made sure that he placed obstacles in the paths of the dreamers to distract them, cause them to doubt, or even abort their dreams.

Joseph was a dreamer whom God called to not only save his Hebrew people but also to become the prime minister of the greatest nation in the world during his time.

Daniel was also a man of God who was able to interpret dreams, and he was not only able to minister to the king of Babylon but to prophesy the events that would occur in the near and distant future.

God spoke to the apostle Paul many times through dreams and visions by the Holy Spirit. These dreams would lead him to places where the Gospel could be preached to the unsaved world.

John on the isle of Patmos received from God the Word from Jesus that would prepare those of us who believe for the day of our Lord's return.

God tells us in the Book of Joel that old men will dream dreams and young men will have visions (see Joel 2:28). God is faithful to His Word. He is giving kingdom dreams today like never before. God is giving believers kingdom dreams that are designed to help those of us who await the return of our Savior Jesus Christ to be ready when He comes again.

As you read this book by my friend and brother in Christ, Dr. Clinton Baker, please be inspired by the message and testimonies. According to the words and writings of the prophet Amos, God will do nothing until He has revealed it to His prophets (see Amos 3:7).

His Kingdom shall come and His will shall be done on the earth as it is in Heaven. Your kingdom dream shall come to pass if you embrace it, have the faith to believe it, and have the patience to endure until it becomes a reality.

Dr. Ron Kenoly

PREFACE

Where there is no vision, the people perish: but he that keepeth the law, happy is he (Proverbs 29:18).

God is releasing from the courts of Heaven, kingdom dreams to those who will embrace them. These dreams are designed to guide us—like a blueprint—but never take the place of the Architect. These dreams are so important that if we do not have them Proverbs 29:18 declares that we will perish. It is not that we will just have a hard time in life, but we will perish. I do not believe we have always comprehended the seriousness of a dream from God. To follow the dream is to save your own life. My prayer for every person reading this book is that you will cry out to God to reveal to you His kingdom dreams for your life so you can live, thrive, and enter eternity hearing, "Well done, thou good and faithful servant" (see Matt. 25:21).

INTRODUCTION

GOD'S KINGDOM DREAM IN YOU

Yes, your dreams birthed without God's Spirit will die. But kingdom dreams live forever—being fulfilled by your descendants for generations to come.

What is the difference between a kingdom dream and your own personal hopes, wishes, and desires? Kingdom dreams come straight from the throne of God. They emanate power, hope, endurance, and possibility. Regardless of the challenges or attacks, kingdom dreams fight through the difficulties and emerge victorious in the end.

The word *kingdom* implies a king. In God's Kingdom, He reigns. You are not the captain of your own ship or the master of your own household—God is. The dreams He has for you are about His Kingdom within you. He wants to reign in your life so that you and others will experience His Kingdom in all of life. Kingdom dreams explode with blessing and unlimited potential when He rules every aspect of your life.

Some of God's kingdom dreams for you may feel like they have died, but God wants to bring life to His dreams for you. The Holy Spirit is very real in us and very real in the earth right now. First Corinthians declares:

> *But the manifestation of the Spirit is given to every man to profit withal. For to one is given by the Spirit the word of wisdom; to another the word of knowledge by the same Spirit; to another faith by the same Spirit; to another the gifts of healing by the same Spirit; to another the working of miracles; to another prophecy; to another discerning of spirits; to another divers kinds of tongues; to another the interpretation of tongues: But all these worketh that one and the selfsame Spirit, dividing to every man severally as He will (1 Corinthians 12:7-11).*

According to this Scripture, when the Holy Spirit manifests Himself and we yield to His ways, He manifests Himself nine different ways. So if the Spirit of God wants to prophesy or if He wants to heal, He manifests Himself through one of these nine gifts. In the Church, we often seek to limit the Spirit to doing what we want instead of what He wants. God will manifest Himself however and whenever He chooses if the people of God will believe Him to do that. We do not want to offend or grieve the Holy Spirit. Allow Him to manifest, as He will, in your life through His kingdom dreams for you.

In this book, you will see that you have to give up your dreams for His dreams. You must decrease so that He will increase. You must decide to yield yourself to the work of the Holy Spirit in you and through you—as you rise up and as you lie down. Prepare yourself to experience His kingdom dreams through you and in you. Dream and then walk in His destiny for you.

This book is not meant to be a quick read for information; it is a manual you can refer to over and over on your journey to your destiny. There may be times you will not fully understand what you are reading, but as you continue to walk through life, you will have a need and the Spirit of God will use the pages here to guide, encourage, and strengthen you as your dreams become reality.

I encourage you to prayerfully read through this book and watch for keys that will feed your dreams. Ask God to reveal them to you as you need them. My prayer is that these pages will help you to persevere, to continually move forward with your God-given dream, and to change the course of history by turning your dream into reality. Take the time to ask for God's help as you seek to accomplish His plan for your life. Be encouraged by the Book of Philippians, which says, "Being confident of this very thing, that He which hath begun a good work in you will perform it until the day of Jesus Christ" (Phil. 1:6).

Finally, before continuing on, I invite you to join me in this prayer:

> *Father, help me to see the things You have ordained for me. Help me to accomplish the plans You have laid for me. Help me to bring You glory in all that I say and do, and help me to receive from this book the anointing and truths You have placed within these pages. In Jesus' name. Amen.*

Chapter 1

DELIGHT IN THE
LORD THEN DREAM

Set Your House in Order

From early childhood, my mother taught me life lessons related to fulfilling my dreams and achieving my God-given destiny. One of the first lessons I remember had to do with God being a God of order. "God cannot bless anything out of order," she patiently explained, "so you must constantly strive to set your house in order."

My mother was a great storyteller and made the Bible come alive for me as she taught these life lessons from the Scriptures. She took me to Genesis chapters 1 and 2 to teach me God's concept of order through descriptively explaining the story of creation. "If God set order from the very beginning, will He not demand order from us?" she asked. I grew up knowing that order was critical to turning a dream into reality.

My mother did not just teach order; she lived her life that way and taught me to do the same. There are some people who live their lives without order and then run around frantically cleaning up when company arrives unexpectedly. In our house you maintained order and kept not only your room in order but your spirit, soul, and body as well. As I grew up in the Church, this was a sermon I heard over and over, "Get your house in order because you do not know when Jesus will return."

This training helped to get me back on course during the times when it appeared my dreams were not becoming reality. I would remember the lessons of my childhood, "God will not bless what is out of order. He is not a God of confusion and disorder but of peace and order" (see 1 Cor. 14:33 AMP). When my life is really in godly order, things begin to come together by God's doing; I do not have to initiate anything.

Sometimes we can get frustrated because our dream seems to be stifled by circumstances or people, but when we get our house in order, God will breathe new life into that dream. In Ezekiel chapter 37, the valley of dry bones represents how the hope of God's people had dried up. God explains this to Ezekiel saying, "Son of man, these bones are the whole house of Israel: behold, they say, Our bones are dried, and our hope is lost: we are cut off for our parts" (see Ezek. 37:11). Then God continues to explain that He will breathe new life back into them and restore their hopes and dreams by his Spirit (see Ezek. 37:12-14).

Many people have become like that valley of dry bones. They have lost hope in ever seeing their dream turned to reality, but God's life can help them believe again. If you are at this point and you need God to restore your hope, stop right now and pray this prayer with me:

Father, in the name of Jesus, breathe new life into me. Restore my hope in You. Father, help me to see clearly what dream and desires You have placed in me. Now bring people into my life who can help me to learn how to walk in divine order. In Jesus' name. Amen.

There will be times in our walk with God that we may feel utterly discouraged and want to quit. When those times come we must make sure we are operating in a spirit of order. The Holy Spirit is there to help us keep our lives in godly order, but we have to make sure we do not ignore His promptings. God will never turn a dream into reality as long as things in our lives are out of order. Let's begin by making sure the desires of our hearts are in order.

WHERE IS YOUR DELIGHT?

In order to bring a kingdom dream into reality, we must first understand that God put that dream in our spirit. When we talk about our *spirits*, we mean "heart." *Leb* in Hebrew means "heart," but it refers to the whole inner person, not the organ pumping blood throughout our bodies. Everything within us—mind, will, emotions, and spiritual life—is called our heart. It is the center of our whole being.

Scripture says, "Delight yourself in the Lord and He will give you the desires of your heart" (Ps. 37:4 NIV). The first thing we must do is to delight ourselves in the Lord. I want us to get this straight because many times we try to go after our desires without first delighting ourselves in the Lord.

In order for God to do what He needs to do in your heart and bring forth what He has placed in your heart, you must first delight yourself in Him. Nothing happens without first having a relationship with God who demands to be ruler of your life. As He reigns, you learn how to receive and submit to His kingdom dreams for you.

Relationships are filled with desires. Often those desires are selfish and self-centered. When that is the case, pride hinders God from imparting His desires into our hearts. Pride comes before a fall (sin or transgression) in our lives.

I want to say this because I believe right now as you read these words and trust God, He will cause something to come from Heaven to impart into your spirit supernaturally. God will do something in your spirit that man cannot do. When His desire replaces yours, then kingdom dreams will be birthed in your heart.

In the past, you may have had something in your heart from God. You may have seen it year after year after year, but you said, "God, how in the world can I do all this?" God puts a dream in our heart, but many times we make excuses like:

- I don't have the time.
- There's not enough money.
- My ability is lacking.
- Others will reject or oppose me.
- It's simply not possible.

We say things like, "If I had this, then I would do that. If I had enough people who supported me, then I would do that." I am here to tell you that God saves. Whether He saves by many or by few, God saves. God saves the dreams He inspires and the people in whom He puts the dreams.

Yes, it is warfare. Yes, it is work. When we unpack what is in a dream, we will never find things are easy, passive, struggle-free, simplistic, or foolish. The truth is that within the baggage of God's dreams are articles like hardship, difficulty, trials, tests, struggles, pain, and work. A dream is not winning a lottery. It is not money falling from Heaven. Dreams shape us in the fiery crucible of God's furnace. He forms us on His potter's wheel by forcefully molding and shaping us.

You may have been feeling attacks in your body or trials in your relationships. Your enemies and the enemy of your soul will attack you. It is hard birthing, raising up, and then maturing in kingdom dreams.

When God puts something in your heart from Heaven, the enemy may come after you. Many of you in your heart have been questioning God, asking:

- Why am I going through all this?
- Why am I facing so much?
- Why does it seem like at home, with my child, in my community, and every single place I go, I am facing something?

It is because you are pregnant. If you are not pregnant with something from Heaven, the enemy will not bother you. If you had nothing that was conceived of the Holy Spirit, satan would not bother you.

At times, satan understands you better than you understand yourself. Joseph had a dream that caused everybody in the entire world to be provided for. I am convinced that what God has put in your heart is going to influence many—if you will allow God to do His work in and through you.

Ecclesiastes says, "To everything there is a season, a time for every purpose under heaven" (Eccles. 3:1 NKJV). There is a time in which your dream must come to pass. Some are delaying the dream because they are disobeying the Holy Spirit. We cannot live in the flesh and at the same time have a dream come to pass by God. We must walk in the spirit and live in the spirit. In other words, the dream that is in you is spiritual.

FRUSTRATED? THEN MOVE OVER!

I must tell you that if you have been frustrated because you know what God has put in your heart but it is not happening, you are in the right place. Let me tell you what God is trying to do. He is trying to cut out manipulation and control. Sometimes we try to make His dream happen in our own strength. We try to manipulate and control God and others in order to manifest a dream.

Getting others to help you will not help. Yes, their intercession will help but their agreement with you for God to do this or that will not help. Remember, prayer is praying what God wants, not what we want. Stop enlisting the support of others and begin to ask for their prayers that God's desire would be birthed in you and your desire would die. Are you ready to surrender control of the way or the timing of your dream being realized?

As you go forward with God, His dream in your heart must be pure. God begins to deal with the motivations of what is really in your heart. Surrender what you want. Release what you feel. Change your mindset. Relearn your responses and behaviors. God is doing a new thing in you in order to birth His desires in your heart.

Think of it this way: Every baby requires a womb within which to grow. You are the womb. God's desires are the seed. The dream is the baby, and time is needed for gestation. A mother cannot control or manipulate the gestation process. If she does, abortion or distortion happens. Get out of God's way. Desire what He desires!

At times, we can become so caught up in the dream that we miss Him. We begin to worship our dream instead of focusing on the King of kings. Let me tell you that God will not allow the dream to be bigger than He is in your life. God will block the dream until the relationship is right. At the core of that relationship is God who is in control. He reigns. It is His desire by His Spirit birthing His dream. Get ready for some birthing pains!

KINGDOM DREAMS KEY POINTS

➤ Let go of personal desires and enthusiastically embrace God's desires!

➤ The first thing we must do is to delight ourselves in the Lord (see Ps. 37:3-4).

➤ When His desire replaces your desire, kingdom dreams will be birthed in your heart.

➤ What God has put in your heart will influence others throughout the world.

➤ The dream that is in you is spiritual.

➤ Prayer is praying what God wants not what we want.

➤ You are the womb. God's desires are the seed. The dream is the baby, and time is needed for gestation.

➤ God will not allow the dream to be bigger than Himself.

Chapter 2

~

THE DREAM IS
ABOUT GOD

DON'T BURN YOUR BRIDGES

God puts people in our paths to help us along our way. Those divine appointments are gifts; they are not to be taken lightly or discarded on a whim. Early in my childhood, my mother taught me a very valuable lesson in life that has helped shape my destiny ever since. She mused, "Son, don't ever burn a bridge because you might have to cross back over it."

While it took years for me to understand what she meant, I have discovered that this simple principle has saved me from grief many times over. My mother's bottom line was this: no matter how you are treated, you still need to treat people right.

At times, people may mistreat us and feel as if they have done nothing wrong. Nevertheless, our responsibility is to forgive them from the heart and still respond with kindness. Everyone experiences being hurt by others and having to work through feelings of anger and resentment. We must learn to value people above any mistreatment.

People are like bridges. We never know how God will orchestrate events. He may even use a person who hurt us in the past to move us over the next chasm blocking His dream for us. God may use past offenders as a bridge for us to reach the highway that turns dreams into destiny! When we are hurt, we may be tempted to blame others or God, rather than seeing such moments as opportunities to learn more about ourselves, to grow, and to move forward in forgiveness and love.

The early Christians saw Saul as an archenemy, a threat to their very existence and the dream of God for them. As a Jewish leader, Saul sought to kill every Christian he could lay his hands on. We read about Saul in the Book of Acts:

> *And Saul, yet breathing out threatenings and slaughter against the disciples of the Lord, went unto the high priest, and desired of him letters to Damascus to the synagogues, that if he found any of this way, whether they were men or women, he might bring them bound unto Jerusalem. And as he journeyed, he came near Damascus: and suddenly there shined round about him a light from heaven: And he fell to the earth, and heard a voice saying unto him, Saul, Saul, why persecutest thou Me? And he said, Who art Thou, Lord? And the Lord said, I am Jesus whom thou persecutest: it is hard for thee to kick against the pricks. And he trembling and astonished said, Lord, what wilt Thou have me to do? And the Lord said unto him, Arise, and go into the city, and it shall be told thee what thou must do (Acts 9:1-6).*

The lesson about not burning bridges is clearly seen in the conversion of this great apostle. For the very people Saul once persecuted, he became a bridge to reach their highway of destiny. Can you imagine how these people must have felt about their former persecutor? They felt anger and fear because they did not know if this conversion was a trick. God can change even a former murderer and make him a bridge in His Kingdom.

Even when we are mistreated, we need to remember that the paths we take are ordered by the Lord. The Lord knows what to allow in our lives to cause us to become a bridge or to receive the bridge provided. Sometimes our attitude is not Christlike, and some type of suffering will cause us to humble ourselves before God and man.

Second Corinthians reads, "And lest I should be exalted above measure through the abundance of the revelations, there was given to me a thorn in the flesh, the messenger of satan to buffet me, lest I should be exalted above measure" (2 Cor. 12:7). This thorn, referred to here by the apostle Paul, was an irritation that was designed to bring humility in his life. This was a messenger from satan, a demonic spirit that harassed Paul everywhere he went. Please understand that Paul was speaking about something specific in his life for his situation, and we do not want to be open to all messengers of satan, thinking this might lead to humility.

This harassment kept Paul close to God and tender in his heart so that he could be used as a bridge in God's Kingdom. A bridge serves an invaluable purpose and affects the lives of everyone that comes in contact with it. God needs to keep "bridge believers" in a spirit of humility because of the impact they will have on the dreams of many others. Just think about the damage that could happen if a bridge fails.

Without bridge ministries in the Body of Christ, a lot of plans and purposes would never see fruition. For example, my secretary is a bridge. People never get to me unless they first go through her. Our views of people are often different from the way God sees them. We read in First Corinthians, "Nay, much more those members of the body, which seem to be more feeble, are necessary" (1 Cor. 12:22). In other words, my secretary is my assistant in many areas, but there are many who may overlook the importance of her bridge relationship to the Body of Christ. If we do not discern the importance of bridges, we will miss God's process of turning dreams into reality.

LET GOD BIRTH YOUR DREAM

God is birthing His dream in you and using people as bridges all along your way to move you forward into His destiny for you. How does that happen? A dream is God's desire within us being birthed by His Spirit. God will not allow it to be bigger than He is because this dream is all about Him. Make no mistake about this: everything we do is supposed to be about Him. First Corinthians clearly states that God will not allow any flesh to glory in His presence:

> *But God has chosen the foolish things of the world to put to shame the wise, and God has chosen the weak things of the world to put to shame the things which are mighty; and the base things of the world and the things which are despised God has chosen, and the things which are not, to bring to nothing the things that are, that no flesh should glory in His presence (1 Corinthians 1:27-29 NKJV).*

It is not about you looking good. Most of the time, when you start talking about your dream, people are going to think you are crazy anyway. Jacob thought his son Joseph had lost his mind when Joseph shared about his dreams. (See Genesis chapter 37.)

Some people, like Joseph's brothers, might be intimidated by your dreams. They might be afraid that the dream in you may come to pass. They may plot against you, but if you do not quit and you do not give up, God will make sure that dream happens. Remember that Joseph's brothers—as mean and cruel as they were—became a bridge to Joseph's future. Decades later, they discovered that the very "bridge person" they had tried to destroy became the one who saved their lives and preserved God's destiny for their families.

Joseph certainly did not look like a ruler when he was in the pit, a slave in Potiphar's house, or an inmate in the prison. The Bible says that throughout all of these humiliating circumstances, God was with Joseph (see Gen. 39:2-4;20-23). Why? Because God intended for those dreams He had placed in Joseph to be fulfilled.

GOD OWNS THE SHIP AND EVERYONE ON IT!

Many times we are looking for our ship to come in. I am here to tell you that God owns the ship and all the people on that ship. You need to get on your knees and cry out to God concerning the dream that He has placed inside of you.

I want you to see something incredible in the Bible concerning God's plan and His attention to detail when it comes to the fulfillment of His dream in you. Mary and Joseph were bringing their firstborn, Jesus, to the temple to be circumcised according to the law of the Lord. They first met a devout and righteous man named Simeon whom God had promised would see the Christ before he died (see Luke 2:21-35). As Mary and Joseph marveled over what Simeon had said to them, a prophetess named Anna came up to them. She was there awaiting the promised Messiah.

> *There was also a prophetess, Anna, the daughter of Phanuel, of the tribe of Asher. She was very old; she lived with her husband seven years after her marriage, and then was a widow until she was eighty-four. She never left the temple but worshiped night and day, fasting and praying. Coming up to them at that very moment, she gave thanks to God and spoke about the child to all who were looking forward to the redemption of Jerusalem (Luke 2:36-38 NIV).*

Anna's assignment from God was to intercede that the Messiah would come. You have got to get a hold of this. The dream will not come to pass until you get an intercessor to cry out to God and begin to pray. God will place Simeons and Annas in your life if you will hold onto your dream and not quit when others laugh or ridicule you.

THE STEPS OF A GOOD MAN ARE ORDERED BY THE LORD

> *The steps of a good man are ordered by the Lord, and He delights in his way. Though he fall, he shall not be utterly cast down; for the Lord upholds him with His hand (Psalm 37:23-24 NKJV).*

The Bible says the steps of a good man are ordered by the Lord. But Jesus said in Matthew, "No one is good but One, that is, God" (see Matt. 19:17 NKJV). Is the Bible contradicting what Jesus said? No, it simply means that it is because of God in us that we are good in the first place. No matter what we have been—liars, cheaters, deceivers—if we repent, we can receive not only His forgiveness but also step into our full inheritance (see 1 John 1:9).

God has a covenant, a plan, and a purpose for your life, and He will do whatever is necessary to bring it to pass. He will use whomever He chooses to bridge you through to the next season of your life in fulfilling your dream. There are times when God will bring someone up and pull another down just to show He is God. As it says in Romans, God said, "Jacob I have loved, but Esau I have hated" (see Rom. 9:13 NKJV). Who can fight God?

The Book of Jeremiah says, "Before I formed you in the womb I knew you; before you were born I sanctified you; I ordained you a prophet to the nations" (Jer. 1:5 NKJV). God was telling Jeremiah that he had the authority to do what God had assigned him to do. God already has a plan for you, but you must get in a place where you can hear God and allow God to show you who you are.

MY SHEEP HEAR MY VOICE AND THEY FOLLOW ME

My sheep hear My voice, and I know them, and they follow Me. And I give them eternal life, and they shall never perish; neither shall anyone snatch them out of My hand. My Father, who has given them to Me, is greater than all; and no one is able to snatch them out of My Father's hand (John 10:27-29 NKJV).

The Bible says, "My sheep hear My voice, and I know them, and they follow Me" (John 10:27 NKJV). This is like being in the military; every single step is under His command. In order for this to happen though, you must be in a place where you can hear God.

FROM DREAM TO DESTINY

I am here to tell you that if you have something in your heart that is not coming to pass it is, because you are not in a place to receive instructions from your commander in chief.

In the world, people think you are crazy if you hear voices. However, God's instruction book tells us that His sheep know His voice and they will not follow a stranger (see John 10:1-5). The Bible also warns us to test such voices and be sure that it is the Lord speaking to us (see 1 John 4:1). How do we do this? Read First John chapter 4:

> *By this you know the Spirit of God: Every spirit that confesses that Jesus Christ has come in the flesh is of God, and every spirit that does not confess that Jesus Christ has come in the flesh is not of God... (1 John 4:2-3 NKJV).*

Jesus also assured His disciples that He would provide a way for them—and for those of us who were to follow—to know the truth.

> *However, when He, the Spirit of truth, has come, He will guide you into all truth; for He will not speak on His own authority, but whatever He hears He will speak; and He will tell you things to come (John 16:13 NKJV).*

Sending the Holy Spirit to us is how Jesus fulfilled His promise to all of His disciples when He said, "I am with you always, even to the end of the age" (see Matt. 28:20 NKJV).

So, the Holy Spirit is birthing His dream in you. It is about God and His desires for your life. It is not about you and your self-centered wants. Remember that some people may appear to be hindrances to that dream. Do not let hurt and offense cause you to burn any bridges. Instead, humble yourself. (We will talk more about how to humble yourself in the next chapter.) Then forgive and love. The very ones who seem to oppose you now may be the bridges God uses in the future to help you pass over the greatest obstacles in your life.

KINGDOM DREAMS KEY POINTS

➢ God will not allow any flesh to glory in His presence, so stay humble (see 1 Cor. 1:27-29).

➢ See difficult, hurtful, and offensive people as your opportunity to be humble, forgiving, and loving. Do not burn the bridges of those relationships.

➢ It is not about you looking good; it is about doing God's will.

➢ God owns the ship and everyone on it! God is in control.

➢ God will place Simeons and Annas in your life if you will hold onto your dream.

➢ The steps of a good man are ordered by the Lord (see Ps. 37:23-24).

➢ God will do whatever is necessary to cause that dream to happen.

➢ God says that His sheep hear His voice and a stranger they will not follow (see John 10:1-5).

Chapter 3

≈

ENLARGE THE PLACE
OF YOUR TENT

Sing, O barren, thou that didst not bear; break forth into singing, and cry aloud, thou that didst not travail with child: for more are the children of the desolate than the children of the married wife, saith the Lord. Enlarge the place of thy tent, and let them stretch forth the curtains of thine habitations: spare not, lengthen thy cords, and strengthen thy stakes; For thou shalt break forth on the right hand and on the left; and thy seed shall inherit the Gentiles, and make the desolate cities to be inhabited (Isaiah 54:1-3).

On the inside, many of you are like this desolate barren woman: you feel you cannot possibly bring forth the dream that is within you. There is nothing more humiliating for a woman than to talk about having a child and then find she cannot produce anything. It is the same kind of feeling a person experiences when they know the dream within them is from God, and they know that they are called to do something, but they do not believe they have the ability to do it.

The Bible has good news for those of you who have not yet produced and have not yet brought forth. God says, to those of you who are impregnated by His dream but have not yet given birth— get ready, enlarge the place of your tent, and strengthen your stakes. God is about to do something great in your life! And when He does, stay humble!

STAY HUMBLE!

My mother, to this day, will still tell me to be humble when things are going well. I used to wonder why she would say this to me so often, but now I know the Holy Spirit was forewarning me. God may be working mightily through you, but you will always have to guard your heart against a spirit of pride. Yes, His kingdom dream for you is to enlarge your tent, but that requires humility. In the process of growing, expect more trials!

As you expand your tent, you may be tempted to think that you are accomplishing the dream and may begin to take personal credit for what God is doing. "And whosoever shall exalt himself shall be abased: and he that shall humble himself shall be exalted" (Matt. 23:12). This verse has impacted me so greatly that when things are going wrong, I know I need to humble myself.

Humility is simply submitting in my heart to the plans and purposes of God. We do this by reading the Word of God and adapting our lives to the teachings found in it. We also have to submit ourselves to the work of the Holy Spirit. Sometimes our attitudes do not reflect humility, even though we obey outwardly. We may complain and murmur in our hearts about what we are required to do, and this becomes a serious thing in the sight of God.

Do not complain; humble yourself. As it says in First Corinthians, "Neither murmur ye, as some of them also murmured, and were destroyed of the destroyer" (1 Cor. 10:10). Complaining opens the door to a spirit of destruction. This is a warning to us that demonic spirits can destroy us if we do not learn how to govern our mouths as we are moving toward the fulfillment of our kingdom dream. In order to enlarge the place of our tent, we must humble ourselves in God's sight. Then He will expand our dream and cause an explosion of growth to accompany our endeavors.

Humility lets God do whatever He wants. First Peter says, "Humble yourselves therefore under the mighty hand of God, that He may exalt you in due time" (1 Pet. 5:6). God promises to exalt us by His mighty hand. How strong is God's hand? How much power does God really possess? Isaiah the prophet gives us a small glimpse of His majesty and glory:

> *Who hath measured the waters in the hollow of His hand, and meted out heaven with the span, and comprehended the dust of the earth in a measure, and weighed the mountains in scales, and the hills in a balance?* (Isaiah 40:12)

This mighty and awesome God can do whatever He wants, whenever He wants, and He promises to exalt all who humble themselves under His mighty hand. When God is determined to do something, no one can stop Him. In order for us to see our dreams become reality, we must humble ourselves before Him. It does not matter how humble we look to man, it is what God sees in us that counts.

God promises to exalt all who will walk in a spirit of humility. Sometimes we may try to humble ourselves just to resolve a situation, but this is not what God is looking for. God only exalts what is genuinely humble in His sight. We have to guard our hearts against pride, especially during times of being promoted. It is human nature to want to look good and be seen a certain way.

There are times when—because of how great God's plans are for your life—He will allow more trials, troubles, or injustices to come in order to keep you humble. When trouble comes we become more tender and loving. Consider the truth revealed in the Book of Psalms:

> *They that go down to the sea in ships, that do business in great waters; these see the works of the Lord, and His wonders in the deep. For He commandeth, and raiseth the stormy wind, which lifteth up the waves thereof. They mount up to the heaven, they go down again to the depths: their soul is melted because of trouble. They reel to and fro, and stagger like a drunken man, and are at their wit's end. Then they cry unto the Lord in their trouble, and He bringeth them out of their distresses* (Psalm 107:23-28).

As we can see in these verses, God sent trouble to cause their souls to melt, humbling them so He could bring deliverance to them. This is God's goal for every person. He uses people and circumstances to humble us so that His dream in us can be fulfilled. God hates pride; there is nothing He can do to help us when we refuse to let go of pride. But when we embrace humility, God says, "Enlarge your tent."

PRIDE CAN DESTROY NOT ENLARGE YOUR DREAM

Pride refuses to rely on God for its strength. Pride says, "I will ascend above the heights of the clouds, I will be like the Most

High" (see Isa. 14:14 NKJV). In Isaiah, satan's pride is revealed. I mention this to show how the pride of our hearts can cause our dreams and destiny to be aborted by the hand of God. It is very easy to be influenced by the spirit of pride because this spirit will cater to your agenda and not God's. Pride is a demonic spirit with supernatural ability, which cannot be defeated by intellect. Pride will tell you that you are okay and that everything is lovely, when things are really in shambles. Pride always works to get us to focus on the outward appearance and what others think about us.

Pride will work to create an illusion and to hide its real motive. Thoughts that come to our minds—that tell us how awesome we are, how good we are, or how much better we are—are designed to keep our areas of sin or weakness covered. Pride will always try to get us to cover up or make excuses for our actions, so we will not get right with God or our fellow man.

Have you ever met anybody who is always right? They never make a mistake ever. They did not misunderstand the message; you just did not give the message correctly. If we are honest, we all have areas of pride of which we need to repent. If we say we do not struggle with pride, then we have been bitten by this spirit. If we genuinely want to see our dreams turn into reality, then we have to acknowledge our sin, so that satan does not have permission or authority to stop our dream.

The cure for pride is to humble ourselves by giving God control of our lives. When we ask Jesus Christ to come into our lives and be Lord (ruler) over us, this is the first step of humbling ourselves. Sometimes we declare to others that Jesus is Lord over us, but in actuality, we are still lord. When we manage our own lives instead of asking God to show us what to do, we are still being influenced by the spirit of pride. Proverbs says, "Trust in the Lord with all thine heart; and lean not unto thine own understanding. In all thy ways acknowledge Him, and He shall direct thy paths" (Prov. 3:5-6). Whenever we do not acknowledge the Lord in "all our ways," we are operating in pride. Sometimes we make decisions without asking God what we should do, and this habit becomes a pattern that we must repent of.

Before we explore further how God enlarges our tents, let's stop right now and pray this prayer of repentance:

Father, I acknowledge my sin of pride. Please open my eyes to see all the ways that I am operating in and being controlled by this spirit. In Jesus' name. Amen.

It is important to ask God to fill you afresh with His Holy Spirit, so you can be controlled by Him and not by an ungodly spirit. Now that you see the dangers of this spirit, you can pray regularly for the Father's help to turn your dream into reality.

We do not have any power outside of God to accomplish the assignment that God has given to us. God knows that our dream is too big to fulfill by ourselves and that we need His continual assistance. Pride will sometimes try to convince us that we are at a point where we do not need God now. We think we can handle it. The truth is, we will never become independent of God.

When we begin to walk with God daily and rely on Him moment by moment, we are walking in true humility. When we learn the lesson that without Him we can perform nothing, we will be ready to see all our dreams turn into reality. Jesus speaks about how we can stay humble when He describes our relationship as a branch depending on the vine:

> *Abide in Me, and I in you. As the branch cannot bear fruit of itself, except it abide in the vine; no more can ye, except ye abide in Me. I am the vine, ye are the branches: He that abideth in Me, and I in him, the same bringeth forth much fruit: for without Me ye can do nothing"* (John 15:4-5).

Humility is depending on God to supply everything we need. Even as I am writing, I am depending on Him to supply His words to teach you how to turn your dream into reality. You may have been hurt after depending on someone and find it hard to trust anybody. The remedy for this is letting everything go from your heart that has happened to you. We have to learn from our past errors but not allow them to control our future. Jesus Christ will never fail you when you put your confidence in His ability to manifest your dream.

One thing we all have to face at times is feeling like God is not there or that He is not bringing our dreams to pass. Remember, God sees the end from the beginning, and He knows when we have really repented of pride and really begun trusting Him. When we really trust God, we do not need an explanation. When God has assured us that we are in His will, we can expect some tough times when He alone will be our only source of hope. There are times when our dreams will face a season of darkness and death, and God alone will be our light and life.

We have learned that as we enlarge the place of our tent, we must stay humble and avoid pride so that His kingdom dream can unfold. We must also remember several other important truths.

GET YOUR EYES OFF OTHERS

Maybe you have been watching other people and seeing them live their dreams, and you are experiencing that old green-eyed monster called jealousy rising up in you. I am telling you that there is no reason for that. Get your eyes off them. God says for you to get ready and make preparations because your time is coming!

His Word says that the first shall be last and the last shall be first (see Matt. 19:30). I am here to tell you that God is going to do something greater in you than you have seen in others. God knows what is in you is what is needed for this hour. Keep your eyes on Him and the dream He has placed in you.

Isaiah says to "enlarge the place of your tent" (see Isa. 54:2 NKJV). Let me tell you, if you really believe God is going to do what He says He is going to do, guess what you need to do? You need to start making some statements of faith and putting some feet to your words. You must begin to make preparations to birth this dream.

If God has told you He is about to bless you with a new home, then you need to start packing up your old home. If God has told you that He is about to start you in a particular area of ministry, then you need to connect with the people of God who have a similar ministry and anointing. Stop being ugly and complaining and do something to move toward the dream God has given you.

Isaiah chapter 54 tells the barren woman to make room in her tent for many, many children. Yes, moving toward your dream requires faith, but faith without works is dead. We see this in the Book of James:

But someone will say, "You have faith, and I have works."
Show me your faith without your works, and I will show
you my faith by my works. You believe that there is one
God. You do well. Even the demons believe—and tremble!
But do you want to know, O foolish man, that faith with-
out works is dead? Was not Abraham our father justified by
works when he offered Isaac his son on the altar? Do you
see that faith was working together with his works, and by
works faith was made perfect? And the Scripture was ful-
filled which says, "Abraham believed God, and it was ac-
counted to him for righteousness." And he was called the
friend of God. You see then that a man is justified by works,
and not by faith only (James 2:18-24 NKJV).

EXPECT THAT GOD WILL STRETCH YOU AS YOU ENLARGE YOUR TENT

Another truth to remember is that God will stretch you as you enlarge your tent. Let me tell you about a pattern with God that will help you to understand His mode of operation. Right before He is about to manifest your vision, all hell may break loose in your life. This is because a crisis will help you to know what you really believe. This is your place of wilderness where you have to come out in the spirit of power by locking your hands at the altar of God. It is a place of fasting and prayer.

Think about the people of Israel wandering around in the wilderness. Moses explained what their wilderness experience was all about as they prepared to enter the Promised Land:

And you shall remember that the Lord your God led you all the
way these forty years in the wilderness, to humble you and test

you, to know what was in your heart, whether you would keep His commandments or not (Deuteronomy 8:2 NKJV).

Who needs to know what is in your heart? You do—God already knows! This is the very hour you must encourage yourself with the Word, worship God with all your heart, and stay connected to your commander in chief. People may walk away from you or tell you that you have lost your mind, but God is saying: stand on what you believe; believe what I have told you, and then I will do what I said I would do. When you do not understand everything, that is your time to connect with God.

KNOW THAT YOU ARE TOO FAR ALONG TO STOP NOW

Remember, God is birthing His dream by His Spirit in your life. When God is enlarging you, there may be times when He will stretch you so much that you will say, "I can't take anymore of this." Giving birth causes stretching, which results in pain—birthing pains.

No woman gives birth to a child without experiencing birthing pains. Women, you know what I am talking about. When you start labor you can't just stop. When we had our first child, my wife was experiencing wave after wave of labor pain. At one point, she said, "Stop, I can't do this." I looked at her and said, "Honey, you are too far along to stop now."

I say that to you right now as you prepare to birth the dream God has placed within you: You are too far along to stop now. I know you may want to throw in the towel. I know you may want to quit. I know you may have been lying in a bed of depression. I know you may not feel like pressing on. I am telling you that you are about to bring forth, so don't quit!

God is about to do something great in your life, so don't quit. When every little thing starts irritating you and you think you just can't be stretched anymore, say, "It might be hard right now but the baby is about to come." Say, "I am pregnant with the dream God has placed in me. I am going to go full term and deliver this dream!" Then go and begin to make preparations for your dream to be born!

KINGDOM DREAMS KEY POINTS

- Get ready, enlarge the place of your tent, and strengthen your stakes.

- Resist and reject pride. Stay humble.

- Get your eyes off others and focus on what God has told you.

- Decide if you really believe that God will do what He says He is going to do.

- Make some statements of faith and put feet to your words (see James 2:18-24).

- Right before God is about to manifest your vision, all hell may break loose. Do not run away from the kingdom dream; run to God.

- Your wilderness experience will help you to know what is in your own heart, what you truly believe.

- You are too far along in the birthing process to stop now.

Chapter 4

DIVINE
CONNECTIONS

Don't Quit!

Especially during my teenage years, my mother would act like a coach when she saw signs I was thinking of quitting. Little did I know that the lessons she taught me would help me fulfill many dreams in my life. She used to say, "Clinton, you are not a quitter. You can do anything with God's help." Looking back, I realize that the Spirit of God was building the heart of a winner in me.

In order to see your dreams turn into reality, you will have to develop the heart and mind of a champion. The Bible is filled with words of encouragement and instruction to help you do just that. For example, in Romans we read, "What shall we say then say to these things? If God be for us, who can be against us?" (Rom. 8:31).

FROM DREAM TO DESTINY

God will supernaturally aid us when we stay true to Him in all that we say and do.

Sometimes we may have a poor image of ourselves. This poor image can cause us to walk in doubt and unbelief and hinder God from assisting us in fulfilling a dream. Hebrews says, "But without faith it is impossible to please Him: for he that cometh to God must believe that He is, and that He is a rewarder of them that diligently seek Him" (Heb. 11:6). True faith, which is complete confidence in God and His Word, is required as He acts on our behalf. God is not tricked by our often-superficial faith. We sometimes say words or exhibit actions that seem like faith, but in the depths of our hearts we will still wonder what God is going to do.

Quitters are quitters because they are struggling with possessing a biblical faith. How do we receive this spirit of faith that does not quit? The Bible declares, "So then faith cometh by hearing, and hearing by the word of God" (Rom. 10:17). This verse actually means that when God speaks His Word to us and we hear, receive, and obey it, there will be an impartation of faith that occurs. When this spirit of faith is imparted, it will change a quitter into a confident, bold winner.

THE POWER OF SPOKEN WORDS

When we have the spirit of faith, we will speak what God's Word says with confidence. Second Corinthians declares, "We having the same spirit of faith, according as it is written, I believed, and therefore have I spoken; we also believe, and therefore speak" (2 Cor. 4:13). You might say what does this all have to do with my dream being turned into reality? Everything!

A God-given dream is a word spoken out of the mouth of God. It is a picture or a blueprint of what God wants to manifest in our lives. It starts as a seed and develops until its appointed time to become reality. A kingdom dream is like a woman who is pregnant and expecting her birth to come during the appointed time. As Habakkuk tells us, "For the vision is yet for an appointed time, but at the end it shall speak, and not lie: though it tarry, wait for it; because it will surely come, it will not tarry" (Hab. 2:3). This vision (the dream and word spoken out of God's mouth) will become reality when God ordains it is time. We have to make sure we continue to carry the spirit of expectancy and speak words in agreement with the God-ordained dream, so that there are no hindrances or spiritual abortions.

A good example of the power of our words affecting destiny and lives is outlined in Luke chapter 1. In verses 5-20, we read how an angel appeared to Zacharias, the priest, to tell him that his prayer for his barren wife, Elizabeth, to conceive a child had been answered. However, Zacharias displayed unbelief when the angel announced that his prayer had been answered, and as a result Zacharias was struck mute until the birth of his son, John the Baptist. In my opinion, there would be no Messiah, no Savior without John preparing the way for Him to come. Zacharias' words could have stopped John's birth and hindered the kingdom dream of a Messiah.

Proverbs warns us, "Death and life are in the power of the tongue: and they that love it shall eat the fruit thereof" (Prov. 18:21). Words can bring life to our dreams and help turn them into reality, or they can kill the dream and destiny. What will you do with your dream, the seed with which you are pregnant? Will you feed it, nurture it, and protect it? Or will you neglect, ignore, or reject the seed that God has entrusted to you? The choice is in your hands. The power is in your mouth! If you stand in faith and do not quit, you will see your dream turn into reality.

GOD WILL GIVE YOU STRENGTH

There are times when we may need encouragement and strength to continue on toward our journey of destiny. Isaiah tells us that God will give us power and strength:

> Hast thou not known? Hast thou not heard, that the everlasting God, the Lord, the Creator of the ends of the earth, fainteth not, neither is weary? There is no searching of His understanding. He giveth power to the faint; and to them that have no might He increaseth strength.... But they that wait upon the Lord shall renew their strength; they shall mount up with wings as eagles; they shall run, and not be weary; and they shall walk, and not faint (Isaiah 40:28-29;31).

Look again at those verses and note that it is the weary who can receive strength. We all get tired and discouraged at times, but God promises to provide supernatural strength that will remove our tiredness if we wait on Him in faith.

When we are waiting on God, there should be an expectation and a hunger for His presence. God will impart supernatural strength to those who are willing to wait for Him to manifest His presence. During the course and stages of our dream development, we will need to learn how to wait on God to divinely energize us, so that we can carry out His plans and purposes. If we do not learn this process of drawing strength, we will develop a quitting mindset and began to lose momentum toward fulfilling our destiny.

How to Protect the Dream

The enemy may try to bring quitters to connect with you to slow you down. Those who walk after the flesh will slow your progress and hinder your dream from progressing. As Galatians reveals, "But as then he that was born after the flesh persecuted him that was born after the Spirit, even so it is now" (Gal. 4:29). So even now those who walk by their human power will cause a strain and blockage to God's Spirit. Jesus was manifest God in the flesh, but even He could not do mighty works in the presence of unbelief. Unbelief includes when we stop believing what God's Word states or stop trusting Him to fulfill His dream in us.

Know that when this kingdom dream is birthed in you, you still must protect it. When Jesus was born, He had to be protected. When it comes out of the spirit realm, God will begin to give you the details of how to work it out in the natural. You have to make sure during the time when it is birthed that you protect the seed— the vision, the dream. How do you do that?

See Yourself as God Sees You

I want to tell you that you can hinder your own destiny because of how you see yourself. In other words, you need to see yourself as God sees you, or you will hinder what God is trying to do in your life.

The people of God could have entered the Promised Land, but they had a poor self-image of themselves. Numbers chapters 13 and 14 tell the story of twelve men who were sent to spy out the land. Only two (Joshua and Caleb) said, "We can take the land." The others said, "We cannot because we are like grasshoppers."

God saw them as mighty warriors ready to move into and possess their Promised Land, but they saw themselves as grasshoppers. They had such a poor self-image that they were ready to give up on their God-given dream.

You may be like these men and say, "I can't see myself going there." But the Spirit of the living God is constant, and I will tell you that signs and wonders will follow you if you just follow the Word. Joshua and Caleb believed what God said about them, and believed He would do what He said He would do, and they stepped into their full inheritance.

As you read the account of Joshua and Caleb, realize how essential it is that you see yourself as God sees you, and do not receive the negative reports of those who cannot see or believe in the dream. Your inheritance depends on it!

> But My servant Caleb, because he has a different spirit in him and has followed Me fully, I will bring into the land where he went, and his descendants shall inherit it.... Except for Caleb the son of Jephunneh and Joshua the son of Nun, you shall by no means enter the land which I swore I would make you dwell in.... But Joshua the son of Nun and Caleb the son of Jephunneh remained alive, of the men who went to spy out the land (Numbers 14:24,30,38 NKJV).

Connecting With Covenant Partners

Another way to protect your vision is to be careful with whom you connect. Many of you may have compromised and connected with other people who are of the wrong spirit. One wrong association can contaminate the vision. When you are accelerating in your vision, you cannot have people around you who remain sorrowful, negative, or do not understand and care about the vision. Moses needed men like Joshua and Caleb around him.

God will bring covenant partners to you to help protect your vision. Do not judge these people in the natural. They may not look outwardly impressive, but they have what you need to protect and advance your dream. The Bible says we have these treasures in earthen vessels (see 2 Cor. 4:7). The help you have been praying for is inside of someone whom God will send your way. Covenant relationships will cause you to accelerate in your dreams.

Connecting With Visionaries

God will connect you with other visionaries. Your vision is supernatural, which means that it has nothing to do with what you have or do not have. Often though, we nearly abort the mission when we cannot see where the finances or the people will come from. God will send you other visionaries that have walked the path you are just beginning. They will encourage you with their testimonies of how God has provided for them. God will send them to help you protect the vision that He has put in you and to reassure you that He will empower you to do what He has told you to do.

Two Words of Caution

God will eliminate those who come between you and Him. You may have a cheerleader in your life—someone who is always saying everything will be all right. But if, after a while, you come to depend on him instead of God, God will cut this person off. God will send you prophets and others to advise you, but He must always remain your final source.

You may have to go through rejection. Every great visionary has experienced rejection and even betrayal. Jesus was despised, rejected, and betrayed (see Isa. 53:3). One of the most powerful prayers you can pray is that God would reveal the associations in your life that are ultimately dangerous to the birth of your vision and the fulfillment of your dream. The quicker you release such relationships, the faster you will advance toward your kingdom dream.

Connecting With Intercessors

God will send you those who will pray and fast and intercede for breakthrough. The prophetess Anna was interceding for the Christ to come forth. She knew the Word and what was happening based on natural times. The Messiah had been born, and she knew she needed to intercede for His protection. In other words, God needed people to be obedient to fast and pray to make way for the Messiah to come. The same is true for the dream in you.

The Importance of Your Relationship With Your Spouse

I love my wife and she is a blessing in my life, but we have been through some issues together along this journey. I am here to tell you that if your marriage is to be anointed, you will have to go through some difficulties in order to reach the place where you can walk toward the dream God has given you together.

Marriage involves taking the two visions God has birthed in you individually and allowing Him to make you one flesh. Those two visions will each try to dominate until the Spirit of God causes the two to become one (see Gen. 2:24). That is why the enemy tries to get you to bicker and tries to breed strife. If he succeeds, he can kill the true vision God has given you as a couple.

Can two walk together unless they have agreement? (See Amos 3:3.) How can you advance toward your dream if there is strife and confusion in your primary relationship at home? Men, you are the head and the visionary of your household. Your wife is there to help you. But if you cannot see clearly where you are going, you will cause your spouse and your household to be in confusion. The head cannot go one way and the body the other way.

Know this: the dream, the vision that God has placed in you includes the help and support of your spouse. Your wife is your key intercessor, your chief encourager, and your strongest supporter. Without her, you will advance very slowly if at all.

God has placed the two of you together for a two-fold purpose. In the natural, it is to produce godly offspring (see Mal. 2:15). In the spiritual, it is to birth His kingdom vision and protect it as it matures and grows. This is your most important divine connection in life, but you should also watch for others whom God will bring alongside to help you birth and protect the dream He has placed within you.

Kingdom Dreams Key Points

- Don't quit. God will provide divine connections for you to move forward.

- Learn how to wait on God.

- Speak life not death. When negative words and thoughts arise, silence them.

- After the dream is birthed, you must protect it so that it can mature and grow.

- One way to protect your vision is to be careful with whom you connect.

- God will connect you with other visionaries to encourage and reassure you.

- God will eliminate those who come between you and Him.

- Every great visionary has experienced rejection and even betrayal.

- God will send you those who will pray, fast, and intercede for breakthrough.

- The dream God has placed in you includes the support of your spouse.

Chapter 5

I Have a
Kingdom Dream

Doing Things for the Right Reasons

"Son, always do things for the right reasons." As a child, I did not clearly see the point my mother was trying to make with this firmly spoken warning. As I grew up and did things just to be seen or heard, that little voice would whisper, "Son, always do things for the right reasons." I would try to ignore that voice and attempt to justify my words or actions, but in my own heart I knew my motives were not pure.

There is an old saying which I remember hearing as far back as I can remember: "You can fool some of the people some of the time, but you can fool God none of the time." The Book of Hebrews makes this point biblically clear:

> *For the word of God is quick, and powerful, and sharper than any twoedged sword, piercing even to the dividing asunder of*

soul and spirit, and of the joints and marrow, and is a discerner of the thoughts and intents of the heart. Neither is there any creature that is not manifest in His sight: but all things are naked and opened unto the eyes of Him with whom we have to do (Hebrews 4:12-13).

The living Word of God has the ability to evaluate our deepest thoughts and true intentions. Sometimes we think we can hide our motives and pretend to be right before God and man. However, the Bible declares, "But if ye will not do so, behold, ye have sinned against the Lord: and be sure your sin will find you out" (Num. 32:23). And Proverbs explains the consequences of trying to cover up instead of confessing our sins. "He that covereth his sins shall not prosper: but whoso confesseth and forsaketh them shall have mercy" (Prov. 28:13). In order to see our dreams become reality, we have to be open and honest with God, while genuinely turning from sin. Sin will hold up everything God has promised us.

We must also realize we will make mistakes along this journey toward seeing our dream become reality. There are many dangers that have to be avoided on the road to fulfilling our dreams. There may be times when we will take a wrong turn, but even then God will help us get back on course if we will admit our mistake and turn back to Him. Mistakes are a part of the journey, but thank God we have a guide who knows where we are going and how to get us there.

The Book of John promises, "Howbeit when He, the Spirit of truth, is come, He will guide you into all truth: for He shall not speak of Himself; but whatsoever He shall hear, that shall He speak: and He will shew you things to come" (John 16:13). The Holy Spirit is there to guide all those who have accepted Jesus as their personal Lord and Savior. The more we learn how to be led by the Holy Spirit, the more we will avoid unnecessary trouble.

DOING THINGS IN THE RIGHT SEASONS

When we were growing up, God put people in our lives who would help us reach physical, mental, and spiritual maturity. I still remember the lessons I learned at my mother's knee and from the teachers and spiritual leaders who spoke into my life. As we begin to mature spiritually, God brings people to help us move toward our destiny during the different growth seasons of our lives. We have to understand the time that God has ordained for each of these people to be with us and be thankful for what they have sown into our lives. Ecclesiastes reminds us, "To everything there is a season, a time for every purpose under heaven" (Eccles. 3:1 NKJV).

However, we also need to be aware of the fact that when one season ends, another begins. If we do not realize when a time or season has passed, we will begin to stagnate instead of grow. Refusing to change when a season is over will kill the dream. God will help us if we have the desire to change. Sometimes we are afraid of what change may hold, but nevertheless change must come. When it is time for change there is absolutely, positively nothing that can stop it besides you.

There are those of you reading this who need to grow and change in order for your dream to be fulfilled. There are others who need to realize you are trying to hold onto a relationship that needs to change in order to see your God-given dream turn into reality. Stop right now and ask God to help you see if a season has changed in your life. Then ask Him to give you wisdom in how to implement that change.

Many times the enemy will challenge us to try to shake us, but God will not leave us undefended. Jesus made a promise to His disciples that applies to us today. "Teaching them to observe all things whatsoever I have commanded you: and, lo, I am with you always, even unto the end of the world. Amen" (Matt. 28:20). When God declares "Amen" at the end of a statement, He is saying it is already done and cannot be changed. There is an "Amen" attached to every God-given kingdom dream.

My Kingdom Dream

I have a God-given kingdom dream. I have shared the basic principles of what this means in the first few chapters of this book. In the next few chapters, I will walk you through my own personal experiences as I journeyed toward the fulfillment of my kingdom dream to encourage you as you make your own personal journey toward your kingdom dream.

As I was praying about this whole concept of a kingdom dream, what came to my mind was that the kingdom dream is something God has placed within each of us. A kingdom dream is not birthed out of the mind of man but conceived by God and planted deeply in the heart of man. I had begun to feel an urgency to share what I had learned and experienced concerning fulfilling the kingdom dream with others. I was becoming more and more aware of how the kingdom dreams of others would affect mine and how mine was interwoven with theirs.

The Lord impressed on me to do a conference focusing on kingdom dreams. As I began praying about how this was all going to come together, my thoughts focused on how critical it was to have the right worship team. It had to be team with a kingdom heart that would set an atmosphere of worship for this conference, which would encourage the birth of things in the Spirit. I asked the Lord to give me guidance and wisdom in how to accomplish this.

I connected with an overseas promoter named Elliot Skinner. I started to share what I felt we needed and suggested a group that had ministered to me personally through their high level of worship. He stopped me in the midst of the conversation and told me he had someone he thought I needed to talk with about this. I was really bothered by this because my heart was set on this other group.

A word of caution here: I nearly allowed my personal preference to get in the way of a divine connection God had put in place for me. Notice I said I had my heart set on a certain group. God's heart, however, was not only for the success of this conference but to accomplish His purposes in my life. A true divine connection always involves so much more than what we initially see.

Watch for Divine Connections and Be Open to Possibilities

There are several keys to achieving a kingdom dream. I want to share my experience to show how these keys worked in my life. I have already touched on the first key, which is to watch for divine connections and be open to possibilities you have never even considered. If you are not alert, you could miss an all-important divine connection and delay the fulfillment of your kingdom dream.

To return to the story, Elliot was persistent about his idea so I asked him who this person was that he was so sure I needed to connect with. He told me I needed to talk to Dr. Ron Kenoly. As I heard his name I was reminded of a prophetic word, which my secretary had given me back in 1995, "You are going to meet Ron Kenoly, and the two of you are going to become friends." I dismissed it at the time thinking, "Ron Kenoly is on the cover of *Charisma Magazine,* and everybody is playing his music." I have to be honest, I felt like Sarah when the angel said she would have a baby at her advanced age. I laughed just as she did.

When this promoter suggested meeting Ron Kenoly, the Holy Spirit reminded me of this prophetic word and then asked me, "Do you want what is popular, or do you want your destiny? What is it that you really want?"

Realize God Will Go Out of His Way to Confirm His Plan

The second key to achieving a kingdom dream is to realize God will go out of His way to confirm His plan. He may bring to your remembrance a prophetic word—or an incident from your past—that encourages you to move forward even when you do not understand why.

I had been praying for years about divine connections and destiny. I had prayed about this conference and told the Lord that I did not want to do anything or bring anyone in unless it was His will. God made sure I knew this was His will! I told Elliot to go ahead and set up a meeting with Ron Kenoly.

I soon discovered selecting a praise team was only part of what was involved in putting this conference together. I had not done a major event like this before. I had done small events but nothing on such a major scale. We had a place with a seating capacity of about 2,500 people. We were expecting that many for this event, and we did not have much time to organize everything.

I had been praying and fasting about this particular conference, and the Lord gave me the dates of June 10-11, 2006. I also prayed, "Lord, not only do I want You to orchestrate the whole event but bring to the meetings those who are ordained in this area of kingdom dreams."

Elliot called to tell me that Ron would be in Europe on those dates. As a matter of fact, Ron was scheduled to be in Europe for thirty days so there was little chance he would leave Europe to do a two-day conference in the States and then return to Europe. Elliot suggested that we look at some other dates.

I knew we were supposed to do the conference on those dates, so it crushed me to learn that Ron would be in Europe then, especially after having the prophetic word regarding him brought back to my mind. Even as I was hearing this news, in my heart I was thinking, "I know what God said and this is what I am standing on."

I left my office and walked outside feeling physically and emotionally tired. I began to pray and talk to the Lord about what I was feeling, reminding Him of what He had told me. "Lord, I do not want to do this anymore. I am tired of trying to make it happen. Every door that needs to be shut—shut it, every door that needs to be open—open it. You said the doors You open no man can shut, and the doors You shut no man can open. It is all up to You. This is Your conference."

Even When Things Seem Impossible for Man, They Are Possible for God

The third key in pursuing your kingdom dream is to remember that even when things seem impossible for man, they are possible for God. Do not waver or doubt, and do not underestimate the power of God to accomplish what appears to be impossible for man. You can miss a divine opportunity if you fail to stand your ground.

As I finished praying, I looked up to see my secretary running down the stairs toward me. She said our promoter had just spoken to Ron Kenoly's secretary who said he would be coming to our conference! I took the phone and heard Elliot say, "Ron will come. He is turning down some other nations that called him because the Lord told him not to go to these other nations."

When Ron Kenoly arrived on June 10th for our conference, he stepped out of the vehicle and said to me, "We meet again. We met once before at the Spartanburg concert." My mind flashed back to an event he had come to in 1995.

It was a major event where all the leaders of Spartanburg had gathered together. Though our church was small at the time, three members of our praise team were asked to sing backup for Ron Kenoly for this event. We were so excited about this opportunity and looked forward to this event.

At the end of that service, Ron called all the area leaders down to the front of the platform saying, "I want to pray for every leader." In my heart, I did not feel like a leader, but my secretary encouraged me to go for prayer. I was the last person to get up out of my seat and go down to the front. The line stretched from the top of the place all the way around this kind of circular stage, and I was the last person at the end of this long line.

Ron prayed for everyone, finally getting to me. As he prayed for me, he was looking at me and I was looking at him as if we knew each other, but I knew we had never met. I knew my spirit man and his spirit man already knew one another—even though there was no conversation; no words were exchanged.

After the event was over the praise team members came to me and asked, "Pastor, do you want to go backstage to meet Ron?" They looked at me strangely when I replied, "I really don't think I am supposed to. He has been out here all this time. We need to just let him go." Many times over the years I have questioned whether I missed destiny. Should I have gone back there to see him that night? But in my spirit, I had felt restraint, and each time I wondered about it, God confirmed that it was not the time or the place.

So when Ron arrived June 10th for our conference, and he remembered the time we met in 1995, I knew for sure that he was here for more than this conference. I felt like we already knew one another, and as soon as we started talking we found there were many things we had in common. God had brought Ron Kenoly into my life to be part of this new season I was about to enter.

Listen to Your Spouse

The fourth key in pursuing your kingdom dream is to listen to your wife so you will not have to apologize later when she is right. Before I left to meet Ron, my wife said to me, "Dr. Ron is going to come to our house to eat." I looked at the itinerary, went through the list of all we had to do before the conference, and told her there was absolutely no time to bring him back to the house. She looked at me, smiled and said, "I am telling you, he is going to come to this house, sit down at our table, and eat with us." My final words to her were, "You can think whatever you want, but I know what we have got to do."

Later, on the way to the hotel Ron and I stopped at a local store. When he came out of the store, he said, "I'm hungry. How far do you live from here?" I told him it wasn't far and then started to list all the things we still had to do before the conference. He stopped me saying, "I am going with you. Let's go to your house."

As Ron got into my car, I was thinking, "My wife is going to say I told you so." Then all of a sudden I started telling him about all the warfare and attacks I had been going through. He listened to me and then said something I will never forget. "A long time ago, I found out it is the baby lions that you have to worry about. Those old lions, they just growl. They can't bite you; they just make a lot of noise. I made a decision that I won't let them bind me or confine me. I am just going to do what I am supposed to do." This so stirred my spirit that I did not say another word for the rest of the drive.

When we arrived at my house, I entered saying, "Honey, I am home. Guess who is here for dinner?" Of course, my wife had dinner laid out on the table and a place prepared for Ron. She smiled as she led us to the dinner table. Later, I had to apologize to her for not acknowledging the prophetic gift in her. We ate and fellowshipped and ended up worshipping together and talking about what the Lord was doing.

Don't Doubt

The fifth key in pursuing your kingdom dream is when you have done what God has told you to do, do not doubt yourself— even if things do not turn out the way you thought they would.

We arrived at the conference venue right at the last minute. I was really excited because I knew God had put all of this in my heart to help people understand that if God has placed a dream in your heart, He will bring the provision and the people to make it come to pass. I was to speak on how they were not to worry about money or people, just do what God is telling them to do at this moment. I was expecting people who think their dream is never going to come to pass and fellow leaders to be there so I could encourage and minister to them.

As the conference was about to start, I looked out over the audience to find the building was not even half full. A mix of emotions flooded my mind. I was discouraged and hurt because I knew that it should have been full. Ron peeked out from behind the curtain and said we are going to be obedient and do this. So he opened the conference, while I was backstage crying and talking to the Lord.

"Lord, all I want to know is have I pleased You? All I want to know is did I do exactly what you wanted me to do? Nothing else matters. Regardless of how this goes, I just want to know I have done what You asked." I was doubting myself on so many things like securing this venue, spending all this money, and thinking I could bring people together and encourage them.

Right at that moment, Ron called me out onto the stage. I was wiping tears from my eyes as I stepped out, and as I looked into his eyes I saw his heart break. Then he said to me, "Have you got your faith together?" All I could do was nod my head. Then he spoke these powerful words to me, "You did exactly what the Lord told you to do, and the Lord is pleased with you." Then he turned to the audience and said, "Everybody, let's just thank God that Dr. Baker has been obedient and done exactly what God has told him to do." That's all I wanted to know.

We held the conference for two nights. Ron and I talked later and felt that God was going to move powerfully on the visions and dreams of the ones who came. At the close of the conference, Ron said to me, "God is going to begin to move quickly because you pressed through." After this conference, when I called Ron to talk he said to me, "Anything you ever become part of I will stand with you. You are a man of faith. I know you follow the Spirit so just let me know." This was the birth of our friendship. I thank God for bringing Ron into my life right at the moment I needed that divine connection.

I am the type of person that if I know God wants me to contact someone—or if someone strongly comes to mind—I will call that person. I call Ron anytime the Lord impresses on me to do so. I can count on my hands how many times I have actually called Ron, but whenever I do there always comes a certain point where he will say, "I know this is God." When his mother passed away, God would not leave me alone. I did not know what had happened, but the Lord said to call Ron. I called and he told me of his mother's passing. A few months later, when my father had passed away and I was grieving, Ron called me. God was deepening our relationship and showing me the value of His divine connections.

KINGDOM DREAMS KEY POINTS

- Always do things for the right reasons.

- Always do things in the right seasons.

- Watch for divine connections and be open to possibilities you have never even considered.

- Realize God will go out of His way to confirm His plan.

- Even when things seem impossible for man, they are possible for God.

- Listen to your wife so you won't have to apologize later when she is right.

- When you have done what God has told you to do, do not doubt yourself even if things do not turn out the way you thought they would.

Chapter 6

A WORD ABOUT PURSUING

THE HEART OF GOD

by Dr. Ron Kenoly

First a Word About Dr. Ron Kenoly

This chapter is very special to me because of a special vessel in the Kingdom of God named Dr. Ron Kenoly. When I was commissioned by the Lord to hold this "Kingdom Dream" conference, I was very hesitant to bring in known ministry gifts because of my lack of trust for "celebrity" ministers. I had met quite a few and did not think there were any left who would not charge you an arm and a leg—until God brought Ron Kenoly. It is not that I do not want to bless ministers of the Gospel because I am also a minister, but some have gotten greedy for money as the Scriptures warn.

I am not introducing Ron Kenoly to many of you because he is known all over the world, but I want you to know from my personal kingdom connection and friendship that he is a man after God's own heart. He is not perfect and has made many mistakes, but who hasn't? However, he will repent and do what God requires, so please be prayerful as you read and receive the next few pages from Dr. Ron Kenoly.

Clinton C. Baker

MY OWN KINGDOM DREAM

I remember those two conferences in Spartanburg, but I have to go back several years before that to show you how God prepared me to follow my own kingdom dream. It was in August of 1982 that I had what I feel was a divine encounter with God, but my journey started even before that.

For the better part of ten years, I had been living in the Los Angeles area, but Los Angeles was killing my marriage so I made a decision to move to Oakland, California. At the time, I had a successful secular music career working with four major recording labels, but I was at a point in my life when I knew I needed to get back on track with my wife and with God.

We moved and began attending Missionary Baptist Church in East Oakland. As I spent time with the Lord, I started writing Scripture choruses and songs from right out of the Bible. I knew that these were songs that God had placed within my heart, but when I tried to sing and present these songs to the church, they flat out told me they did not feel this type of music was appropriate for the church.

At that time there was no real genre in Christian music called praise and worship, which is what I was writing and singing. I did not know anyone else who was writing or singing this kind of music in the churches I was attending or in the churches that I was familiar with. They were songs that were right out of the Word of God.

This music burned in my heart, but when I tried to get a contract with some of the Christian record companies, not one of them was interested. I wrote letters to every major Christian record company that was around at that time, and there was just total rejection. I got one letter from Benson Records telling me they were not interested in any new material or any new artists. I was broken-hearted and feeling totally rejected.

GOD IS IN CONTROL

About that same time, one of my brothers got into trouble with the law and was sentenced to do time up in the Washington State Penitentiary. I would go up there to see him, and one time I found he had told the chaplain that I was a singer. I began to sing these songs, which God had given to me, to those who were incarcerated. I knew God had given me something really special because when I sang these songs, they began to minister to those hard-core, professional criminals. I wasn't sure what, but I knew that God was doing something special in my life.

That chaplain told other chaplains and before long I was singing at institutions all up and down the West Coast of America. I sang these songs of worship in prisons in Oregon, Washington, California, and Nevada. From there it expanded into parachurch organizations, Full Gospel Business Men's meetings, and things of that nature. I still never sang in a church and the record companies still did not accept me either, but God was using me in ways I had never experienced before.

A Divine Encounter With God

In August of 1982, I went across the street into the little Four Square Church that I was now attending. It was a Saturday night and I was feeling really low—rejected, disappointed, and discouraged—because my music was not being recognized by the people who could make something out of it and who could advance it in the music industry. I was just like every other singer; I wanted a record deal and it just wasn't happening. Publishers were not interested, record companies were not interested—even the churches were rejecting me.

So I locked myself in this little church on a Saturday night. I sat down at the piano and began to play every song that I could remember that God had given me since this all started. I played and sang songs of worship, songs of love, and songs of praise. I knew enough not to be angry at God, but I was confused and hurt and knew the Word said He invites us to "come, let us reason together" (see Isa. 1:18). I wanted to reason with Him about what was going on with my music.

I said, "God, You are the One who put these songs in my heart. You are the One who gave me the love and the desire to sing, and I have written these songs and nobody seems to want them so I am giving them back to You." I sat at the piano and worshipped and sang for at least two hours. I don't even remember how or when but I left the piano and found myself laying face down, prostrate on the floor in a pool of tears, just worshipping and loving on God. It was at that moment that I realized I had touched the heart of God.

When I got up off of that floor, it no longer mattered if the record companies and the publishers were not interested in me. It did not matter if the church was never going to let me sing these songs there. None of those things mattered anymore as I realized I had just touched the heart of God with my worship. The best way I can describe it is I could feel the love and the favor of God over my life and over what I had done. I had touched His heart, and when I got up off the floor nothing else mattered anymore.

As I walked out of that building and started across the street back toward my house, right there on the corner of 64th and Bancroft in Oakland, California, I heard a voice calling my name. I cannot tell you if it was an audible voice or not, but I heard my name—Ron. I answered with a question, "Lord, are You calling me?" He said, "Yes, Ron, I am calling you." That is all I needed to know. I did not even need to know what He was calling me to; I just knew that He had called my name. God had spoken to me, approved of me, validated and affirmed me, and I have never been the same since.

That Saturday night in August of 1982, that encounter with God set me on a course of continual pursuit of the heart of God. Praise and worship has been the avenue that has taken me, time and time again, to His heart. This pursuit has made a difference in my life and has caused me to put my relationship with Him above everything else in this world. For the rest of my life, that will continue to be my focus—the praise and worship of God.

KINGDOM DREAMS KEY POINTS

- ➤ God will prepare you to fulfill your kingdom dream through personal encounters with Him.

- ➤ God may place a divine dream in your heart, but not everyone will believe or receive it.

- ➤ Divine dreams, given by Christ, may be a new thing that cannot be compared to anything old.

- ➤ Troubling circumstances are often divine stepping-stones to fulfilling our dream.

- ➤ Those who have been forgiven much are more receptive to embracing kingdom dreamers.

- ➤ Kingdom dreams are signs along earthly highways that ultimately lead to the highway of glory.

- ➤ Rejection from men is designed to get us to totally cling to Christ.

- ➤ When we give the dream back to God, He will bring it to pass.

- ➤ Tears from a broken and pure heart will cause God to move speedily on our behalf.

- A kingdom dream is a calling that needs to be prepared for and embraced.

- Kingdom dreams may be confirmed by man but only validated by God.

Chapter 7

A Progression of
Divine Connections

There Are No "Big I's and Little U's"

I always thought my mother was particularly hard on me when she caught me disrespecting others. At the time, I wondered why this seemed to bother my mother so much. I realize now that God was training me for such a time as this. Today in our society we tend to rate a person's value and respond to them based on own views and opinions. There are times we think of ourselves as having greater worth than the next person. This is what my mother would call the "Big I, Little U" mentality.

The truth my mother continually drilled into me was that everyone is equally important to God. God places His value upon us and does not expect us to devalue others or ourselves. We do not decide where God places us in His Kingdom. Placement is ordered by God to help us fulfill our dream and destiny. First Corinthians clearly explains this concept: "But now hath God set the members every one of them in the body, as it hath pleased Him" (1 Cor. 12:18). God is the Creator of all things and He knows what and who will work best together.

Sometimes we become so self-focused or self-willed that we miss a divine relationship God designed specifically to turn our dream into reality. When we allow this to happen, we miss the treasure God has given us. *Treasure* is defined in *Merriam-Webster Dictionary* as "wealth stored up" or "something of great value." The second definition summarizes the principle my mother constantly tried to instill in me: Everyone is greatly valuable and important to God's plan. Second Corinthians warns us not to overlook this treasure. "But we have this treasure in earthen vessels, that the excellency of the power may be of God, and not of us" (2 Cor. 4:7).

The concept that there are no Big I's and Little U's in God's Kingdom shaped my perception of people from an early age. This lesson has helped me see people the way God does. We have to learn to view things from God's perspective in order to see our destiny fulfilled. God has already selected the way I am to go, as well as the people that will help me on my journey, but it is up to me to receive it. Sometimes we are working against our God-given dream when we reject the people He has placed in our lives.

Sometimes we cannot receive the treasure within an individual because we spend too much time evaluating the outer container. That is like looking at a glass of water decorated with certain pictures on the outside and deciding we do not want the content because of the pictures. There are many people living their lives this way because they have decided that their neighbor does not serve a purpose in fulfilling their dream.

I grew up in a racist era when men were evaluated based on the color of their skin. I would often wonder how many people were missing out on fulfilling their dream because of this prejudicial mindset. My mother and father taught me that there are no Big I's or Little U's in God's eyes. The only thing that really matters is how God sees us, not the opinions of others.

THERE IS ONLY ONE "BIG I"

A "Big I, Little U" society tends to greatly influence the dream or destiny of its people. As people of God, we should not allow this to happen—especially in the Body of Christ. The Book of Romans warns us about not allowing social influences to determine who we are or how we respond to others when it says, "And be not conformed to this world" (see Rom. 12:2). Conforming to this world is developing the same mindset as people who do not know or serve God scripturally. We are called to be different than the status quo; we have been called by God to be a peculiar people.

First Peter describes who we are in Christ: "But ye are a chosen generation, a royal priesthood, an holy nation, a peculiar people; that ye should shew forth the praises of Him who hath called you out of darkness into His marvellous light" (1 Pet. 2:9). This verse calls us a peculiar people. *Peculiar* is defined in *Merriam-Webster Dictionary* as "characteristic of only one." Therefore, as peculiar people, we are one of a kind. We are valuable to God; this is why He only made one of each of us.

Too many times we try to copycat someone else's dream or destiny, but when we do we are not functioning in our peculiar anointing. There is a specialized anointing upon us when we recognize who we are. When we do not despise who God has made us, we can then enter into our dream and destiny with feelings of joy and confidence, not fear and dread. We need to realize there is a specialized anointing on others as well, and not value them just for what they can do for us. Instead we should be seeking to fulfill God's plan and purpose in connecting us.

The only way to fulfill our purpose or dream is to seek God for His wisdom and understanding. God wants us to know His will, but it is revealed only through spending time with Him. Ephesians tells us God wants us to know His will for our lives. "Having made known unto us the mystery of His will, according to His good pleasure which He hath purposed in Himself" (Eph. 1:9). First John assures us that God wants to give us everything we need to fulfill the dream and purpose He has placed within us:

> And this is the confidence that we have in Him, that, if we ask anything according to His will, He heareth us: and if we know that He hear us, whatsoever we ask, we know that we have the petitions that we desired of Him (1 John 5:14-15).

When we recognize that God is the "Big I" and we all fall under Him as "Little U's," we are well on our way to fulfilling the plan of God in our lives. The plan of God will happen just as He intends when we keep the right perspective of the relationship we have with Him and with our fellow man. We must love each other the way He tells us to. We even have to love our enemies in order for God to trust us with the dream He has given us.

JOSEPH'S KINGDOM DREAM

This principle of loving each other is clearly expressed for us as we read about the life of Joseph in Genesis chapters 39-50. Joseph's brothers hated him and tried to destroy him and his kingdom dream. In Genesis chapter 50 we see that Joseph forgave his brothers and was able to be used by God to save a nation:

> *And Joseph said unto them, Fear not: for am I in the place of God? But as for you, ye thought evil against me; but God meant it unto good, to bring to pass, as it is this day, to save much people alive* (Genesis 50:19-20).

The dream and destiny of Joseph would have been destroyed had he not learned the secret of forgiving from the heart. When Joseph allowed God to work His plan, Joseph had a progression of divine connections that led him to the place where God could bring to pass the kingdom dream He had placed in Joseph so many years before. Had Joseph succumbed to bitterness or discouragement anywhere along the way, he might have missed one of the necessary divine connections.

GET READY TO BE LAUNCHED

After the experience I had with Ron Kenoly in June of 2006, I began praying in earnest for more divine connections. I said, "Lord, You bring the people that I am supposed to meet at the right time. You let me know that these are divine connections." Once you ask God to bring divine connections, get ready to be launched.

Suddenly I found I was being launched overseas and into a chain of divine events and divine connections that seemed to happen one right after another. I left for a mission trip not long after the conference with Ron Kenoly. First, I was scheduled to speak at

Martin Buehlmann's twenty-fifth ministry anniversary party. I had never met Martin, but I knew he was a leader over many churches in Switzerland.

When I landed after traveling more than 20 hours, I still had another 30- or 40-minute train ride to the place where I would be staying. I was so exhausted as I prayed, "Lord, I need your strength, but if I could do this differently, and if You could just move things around so it is not such a tough schedule, I would really appreciate it."

With the time zone difference, it was late in the evening when I arrived at my host's home. Everyone wanted to talk to me, but all I wanted to do was go to bed and not engage in long conversation. So I excused myself, went to bed, and fell asleep only to awaken in the middle of the night thinking it was morning. I woke thinking I had slept the entire night, but it was actually only two or three in the morning local time. I jumped up disoriented, thinking I needed to hurry and get ready to go. I ended up waking the man of the house who explained to me that it was three in the morning. He graciously offered to fix me food or whatever I needed. Thanking him for his hospitality, I sent him back to bed after I promised to make myself at home.

THE POWERFUL PRAYERS OF A WIFE

God sent me to that particular house for several reasons. I thought I was there to minister to others, but God sent me to be ministered to by this loving couple. They became like family to me. I was traveling alone, but my wife was back in the States praying, "Lord, just place him in a home that will care for him like I care for him." She was praying this over me and interceding on my behalf. Oh, the awesome power of a praying wife! Do not ever underestimate the power of praying wife!

My hosts, an older couple, were such servants. They took care of me like family and made sure I had everything that I needed. As I experienced their love and care, it reminded me of how I treat people when they come into my home. They made sure I was fed and personally drove me to the places I needed to be. I had prayed, "Lord, all the people that I need to meet, let me meet them." But I still did not understand the impact others might have on me. As I stayed in this home with this loving family, talking and sharing, I developed such a closeness with them that they were able to minister to me even as I prepared to minister to others.

I have to pause here and share that in the midst of all this, I had been personally dealing with major panic attacks and physical attacks on my body. I had begun to think I was not cut out to do this. I had even begun to doubt myself. How can I minister to these people when I am going through all this stuff myself? I had even told God, "I cannot be an apostle to the nations. It requires too much, and I do not think I can take any more assaults on my body." However, I was to learn once again that God has everything under control. First, the family I stayed with ministered lovingly to me, and then I met Martin. Don't ever forget: God is in control, and He is 100 percent for your success.

MEETING MARTIN BUEHLMANN

My hosts took me to Martin Buehlmann's house to meet the man I had heard so much about. I expected him to speak in broken English but found Martin spoke English probably better than I do. When we arrived I heard him talking on the phone in what I assumed was German. As Martin turned and saw me, he said in perfect English, "So Clinton, tell me—how are you doing?"

After we exchanged pleasantries and talked for a little while, he said to me, "I have heard about this kingdom journey you have just had. Tell me a little about it." Time flew by and suddenly it was time for us to go. As Martin was putting on his shoes, he looked at me and said, "Clinton, you are going with me." I was scheduled to ride with my hosts, but Martin said, "We need to go, but I need to share some things with you—so you will ride with me."

As I followed Martin out to his car, I notice that the printed program for the anniversary party mentioned Vineyard churches. I asked if this was referring to the Vineyard churches that were started by John Wimber. Martin replied, "Oh, yes. John Wimber was a mentor and spiritual father to me. As a matter of fact, I went to India when I was a young man and was trained by Bishop Satish Raiborde before coming back to Switzerland to start a church. Bishop Satish was a father to me before I came under John Wimber."

I knew John Wimber had trained prophetically and had prayed years before to meet him and his training staff. I was sad when I heard that John Wimber had died before I had an opportunity to connect with him. But here it was years later, and God was honoring my request by letting me meet one of Wimber's spiritual sons. Isn't it amazing how God delights in giving us the desires of our hearts?

As Martin slid into the driver's seat, he instructed me to take the front passenger's seat. There were other people in the back seat, but he began to prophesy directly to me. "Clinton, the white males, in ministry in the United States have done a disservice to black ministers, but God is going to restore." As I was sitting there—thinking I had already been healed from all the old racist stuff I had gone through—suddenly I began to weep.

Then Martin said the most amazing thing to me. "Clinton, you do not know this, but you are helping me fulfill a dream by your being here." As I was thinking, *What could I possibly do to fulfill a dream for a man like Martin Buehlmann?* Martin explained, "I've always wanted to bring Ron Kenoly to Switzerland for eight hours of worship joining with our Vineyard worship leaders. And you are the man."

God was showing me that divine connections are not always about what that person can do for you to help you fulfill your dream. He will also use you to help them fulfill their dream. Divine connections go both ways—you to them and them to you.

A Tent Full of Divine Connections

When we arrived at the meeting place we walked in together, but I was sure that Martin had things to do to get ready for the meeting. He introduced me to the staff saying, "This is my friend, Clinton. We have been friends now for one hour." Then instead of going off to prepare for the meeting, he began taking me around and introducing me to all these people. We were talking with everybody. He said things like, "See this man right here? We have been friends for 25 years. Clinton, I want you to meet him."

There was a tent set up adjacent to the building where he had arranged a special dinner for all these key leaders attending this celebration. There were supposed to be maybe 100 international leaders but it ended up being closer to 500 world leaders who had come to honor him. Martin sat me down next to a guy with a big, thick moustache. "This is Marcel," Martin said, "He flew in from Jerusalem. He has been my good friend for 25 years. Marcel, I want you to meet Clinton. We have been friends for five hours now."

Then he introduced me to another Marcel, an older man, saying, "This man laid down his life to help establish what you see here today. I have known him over 25 years." Martin continued, "These two men that you are sitting with right now are the top two religious leaders in the world in my book. These are men who have impacted many, many people but they have always been behind the scenes."

As I was sitting at the table with Martin and these two Marcels, I asked the Lord, "What am I doing here? I know these are divine connections, but I do not understand why." Then one of the Marcels (the one from Jerusalem) said to me, "I am going to be in the United States a month or so from now. There is a guy named Rick Joyner, have you heard of him? I have been invited to be part of a round table for prophets and to share some things prophetically with that group." Then he looked directly at me and said, "I don't know what it is you are doing. I just know I am supposed to be a part of it."

As I was looking around at all the world leaders gathered together in this one place—where God had placed me in their midst—I noticed Martin talking to another man. He turned to me and asked, "Have you met Mike Bickle? I was on the platform when he established the first International House of Prayer in Kansas City. He was with us when John Wimber was alive with the

Kansas City prophets." I was sitting in a tent full of divine connections and my head was spinning.

The vision God had given me was so big, and my prayer had been for God to supernaturally build the team and identify those with the specialties needed to fulfill it. Now I realized God was doing it, right here, right now in this big tent. Martin wasn't finished yet. He asked me, "Have you heard of John Paul Jackson? His staff is here with me. They are doing some training while they are here. I am going to introduce you to them because his heart is to build a team to train people concerning kingdom business."

I had asked God for prophets who were pure and to establish the foundation of the apostles and prophets for the dream He had begun to birth in me (see Eph. 2:20). God was establishing an international group capable of speaking into and accomplishing the dream He had placed in my heart. All the way home, I thanked God for all that He had done in such a short time and asked Him to bring clarity now as to what we were supposed to do together.

KINGDOM DREAMS KEY POINTS

➢ Once you ask God to bring divine connections, get ready to be launched.

➢ Don't ever underestimate the power of a praying wife!

➢ Don't ever forget: God is in control, and He is 100 percent for your success.

➢ God delights in giving us the desires of our hearts.

➢ Divine connections go both ways—you to them and them to you.

Chapter 8

Kingdom Dream—The
Next Step

Faithfulness Is a Key Element

Many people are hoping, wishing, and even praying for their dreams to come true, but there is a key element that is missing: faithfulness. In the Book of Matthew, Jesus declares, "His lord said unto him, Well done, thou good and faithful servant: thou hast been faithful over a few things, I will make thee ruler over many things: enter thou into the joy of thy lord" (Matt. 25:21). There is a promotion given to the faithful. Whenever we are consistent in doing what God has asked us to do, there will be a reward of greater influence and authority.

Whenever we are given an assignment by God, though it may seem insignificant to us, it is very important to God. Again in Matthew, Jesus says, "And whosoever shall give to drink unto one of these little ones a cup of cold water only in the name of a disciple, verily I say unto you, he shall in no wise lose his reward" (Matt. 10:42). When we have the right attitude toward whatever God asks us to do, He can cause our dreams to become reality.

Growing up my parents taught me, by word and deed, the rewards of being faithful. They encouraged me from early childhood to work consistently and diligently on whatever task was given and then rewarded me for my faithfulness in completing that task. Sometimes I would be given monetary rewards for a task well done. Then there would be times I received a special privilege, such as being able to go to a friend's house. As I demonstrated faithfulness in the little things, I received more and more responsibility and authority. I believe this helped me gain a better understanding of how God rewards those He deems faithful in His family as well.

Hebrews chapter 11 explains this principle to us: "But without faith it is impossible to please Him: for he that cometh to God must believe that He is, and that He is a rewarder of them that diligently seek Him" (Heb. 11:6). Our view about life must be governed by the Word of God and by His Holy Spirit. Without God's standard, we will not know whether we are on course to fulfill our dreams. We can find ourselves on a road called Lost. Dreams from God are like signs in life, pointing us in the right direction and assuring us that we are making progress. Can you imagine traveling to a new state without any signs posted along the journey? What types of feelings and thoughts would be in the hearts and minds of drivers—panic, fear, frustration, confusion. How could anyone discern whether they were going in the right direction?

Jesus declares in John chapter 14, "I am the way, the truth, and the life: no man cometh unto the Father, but by Me" (John 14:6). One of the keys to faithfulness is being able to stay close to God, even in the hard times. If we remain faithful during these times of testing, God will reward us with a greater measure of influence. There are times when we may feel like our dream will never become reality, but God needs our faithfulness to accomplish the dream that He has put in our spirits.

First Peter says we can trust God because He is a faithful Creator. "Wherefore let them that suffer according to the will of God commit the keeping of their souls to Him in well doing, as unto a faithful Creator" (1 Pet. 4:19). Faithfulness is a part of God's character or nature. He will be faithful to keep every word He has spoken to us, but our part is to let everything in us that is not faithful go through God's refinement process.

THE REFINEMENT PROCESS

This refinement process has been designed by God to remove all things that stop our dream from manifesting in our lives. When God looks at us, first He sees us without our impurities—as a finished product. Then the Holy Spirit reveals the defects or the things in our lives that are hindering our dreams or destiny from being fulfilled. God then puts in place the perfect plan to remove those impurities and move us on toward fulfilling our dream and our destiny.

This process is extremely important to our dream development, because without this refining process in our lives, our destiny would be aborted. Philippians explains God's plan and purpose in us: "For it is God which worketh in you both to will and to do of

His good pleasure" (Phil. 2:13). God will work in us until the dream is turned into reality. God has invested Himself into our dreams, and as long as we cooperate with Him they will come to pass. Faithfulness involves trust and cooperation. As long as we trust and cooperate, God can increase His operations in our lives.

The reason many dreams never become reality is because we are not really trusting or cooperating with God. Ephesians says, "And what is the exceeding greatness of His power toward us who believe, according to the working of His mighty power" (Eph. 1:19 NKJV). The more we trust God, the more His power is available to us to accomplish our dreams.

Hebrews gives us insight as to why we may not be seeing our dreams come to fruition. "For he that is entered into his rest, he also hath ceased from his own works, as God did from His" (Heb. 4:10). Faith and pride are opposites because when we trust in ourselves and do things our way and in our own strength, we block God's work in us. When we start trying to make our dreams happen, we have basically stopped relying on God. Jeremiah gives us a contrast between one who trust himself and one who puts his trust in God:

> Thus saith the Lord; Cursed be the man that trusteth in man, and maketh flesh his arm, and whose heart departeth from the Lord. For he shall be like the heath in the desert, and shall not see when good cometh; but shall inhabit the parched places in the wilderness, in a salt land and not inhabited. Blessed is the man that trusteth in the Lord, and whose hope the Lord is. For he shall be as a tree planted by the waters, and that spreadeth out her roots by the river, and shall not see when heat cometh, but her leaf shall be green; and shall not be

*careful in the year of drought, neither shall cease from yield-
ing fruit* (Jeremiah 17:5-8).

BENEFITS OF TRUSTING GOD

I was determined to be like the blessed man in the Scripture
above, one who trusts God's faithfulness no matter what condi-
tions seem to be around me. When I got home from my trip to Europe, I began earnestly praying for God's guidance concerning all
that He had done. As I sought wisdom from above, the Lord put
an acronym in my spirit: INCF, the International Network of
Christian Filmmakers. I know it had to have come from Him because I have absolutely no training in filmmaking. Filmmaking
was not even on my agenda.

Over the years, I had talked to my brother who owns a studio
in Los Angeles about the need for some good Christian films. But
since my focus was always more toward ministering, I had not ever
really personally pursued this idea of making quality Christian
films. After receiving the idea of INCF in my spirit, I prayed,
"Lord, if this is really from You, bring my brother from LA to me
by the end of the week."

I had recently spoken with my brother and knew he was film-
ing an MTV special with Jennifer Lopez. They were on a very
strict schedule to finish the work, and he had told me that he could
not break away for anything. So I just put the idea of a visit from
my brother before the Lord while really feeling it was impossible. I
should have remembered that what seems impossible for man is
possible with God.

I had prayed that prayer on October 1st. Two days later, I was discussing the INCF idea with my attorney, but I was still unsure about whether or not I should proceed. My secretary interrupted the meeting when she came in crying, saying my father had just had a massive heart attack. As I ran out the door, the Lord told me that my dad was not going to make it. Before I could get to the hospital, my mother called to tell me he had passed. After I arrived at the hospital and was consoling my mom, my brother called from Los Angeles. Even as I was talking with him, it never dawned on me about what I had put out earlier as a request before the Lord.

The significant thing about this is it was my stepfather who had just died. He had raised me, but my biological brother from Los Angeles had lived with our natural dad and did not have the kind of relationship I had with our stepfather. Still my brother said, "Just tell me the arrangements and I'll be there."

The funeral was set for the following Saturday. We were at my mother's house and funeral cars were lined up ready to proceed. Just as we started to get into the cars, a Cadillac came flying up the driveway. My brother popped out and the Lord said to me, "The network is from Me." My brother had arrived at the last minute on a Saturday to attend the funeral. Even though I was filled with grief about my dad's passing, I thought about how God used the death of my dad to let me know that this network is from Him.

INCF IS BORN, NOW WHAT?

The papers were signed and here I was with this brand new International Network of Christian Filmmakers—without a clue as to where it was going or what I was doing. I did know its purpose was to produce good quality, Christian, family-based films. God had gone to a lot of trouble to connect me with my brother, but I knew I needed more than that to move this kingdom dream forward.

I continued to pray for divine connections as this dream began to materialize. Remember, even when we cannot see it, God has a specific plan for success. In the fall of 2006, God began to bring me into contact with some of the most powerful and influential men in the filmmaking industry.

It started with an invitation to a gathering at Bishop Satish Raiborde's home. He had decided he wanted to give me a missions experience of what Indian culture was like, so when I arrived I found the house all set up like it would be in India. As we were all sitting on the floor, in my heart I was praying, "Lord, I only want divine connections. Reveal Your purpose in bringing me here. Lord, I am tired. I know you called me to go to the nations, but I don't feel I am equipped. I don't feel I am strong enough to go."

I had barely finished this silent prayer when Shekhar Kallian-pur stood up, walked over to me, and gave me a prophetic word. He said, "Brother, the Lord says to tell you that I came all the way from India just to meet you. I know this without a shadow of a doubt." Suddenly everything else that was happening all around us seemed unimportant. It was like we were the only two people in the room.

As Shekhar began to explain who he is and what he does, I realized God had indeed set up this divine connection. "I am with Bollywood, the people who make more films than any place on earth," he told me. Now I had never heard of Bollywood. I always thought Hollywood was the biggest film place, but Shekhar explained that Bollywood is much larger.

THE DIFFERENCE BETWEEN DIVINE
CONNECTIONS AND SKILLS

Now the Lord had given us a prophetic word over the years that our ministry was going to be like Joseph's, the dreamer. We all like the end of Joseph's story, but as I started to talk about this film ministry, I discovered what Joseph had to go through before he saw his dream come to fruition. I was mocked, laughed at, and ridiculed. People in the filmmaking business as well as fellow Christians said things like, "You don't know anything about the filmmaking industry; you are an amateur."

My brother was not like that though. Even though I was ignorant in this area, he talked to me and showed respect for what I was trying to do. However, there were other Christian filmmakers I talked with who had a Hollywood mindset. Their advice to me was, "You might want to study up on this before calling any of us. You need to get to a point where you know what you are talking about, then you can call and talk to us about your ideas and your dreams."

I was well aware that I was at the infant stage in this project. At this point, all I wanted to do was find out how to get started with this dream, which I knew God had put into my heart. Instead of helping and encouraging me in pursuit of my dream, these Hollywood experts made me feel discouraged, ignorant, and rejected. So I went back to the initiator of this dream and said, "Lord, You have got to make this happen." We must remember, if God is the initiator of our dream, He is also the provision for it.

The Lord reminded me that Joseph was rejected by his own brothers after he shared his dreams. He said, "I had to send Joseph out into a foreign land to establish him, and then I brought him back to his own people." As Shekhar was explaining who he was and what he did, God was saying, "I brought you Shekhar all the way from India. Like Joseph, you are young and you do not know what you are doing. This is how I did it with Joseph. This is how I am doing it with you."

I realized early on that I did not have the skills to bring this dream to fulfillment. But it did take me a while to learn that, since the dream was from God, it was His responsibility to train and equip me. He would also be the One to bring to me all of those who would help me complete what I could not do. Along the way, I have had to learn the difference between divine connections and working with those who simply have the required skills.

At first, I sought out and brought in people who had the skills to accomplish everything I needed done. But the problem was the devil could send me people who were skilled but had his agenda instead of God's in mind. The devil's agenda is always to steal or kill the vision. God taught me to choose only those whom He sent. It wasn't what was on their resume or the skills they possessed that qualified them to be a part of this project. If God did not send them, I did not want them. At times, this has meant I have chosen people with less experience because God knew that those who seemed more qualified had character issues that would come out later and actually be detrimental to the project.

RELATIONSHIPS DESIGNED TO FULFILL GOD'S PURPOSES

So the INCF filmmaker network has been officially birthed. After meeting Shekhar, a series of other divine connections occurred as I prayed for the next step toward fulfilling this kingdom dream. It was time to begin to grow this dream, but I knew I needed to protect it and follow God's plan, not man's.

God began to bring to my remembrance men I had met in the past but had not understood at that time what the connection was. I thought about an actor I had met years ago who had helped do things for me in my ministry. We always felt we were to do something more together, but at the time neither of us knew what it was. He was an actor who had also struggled as he sought to fulfill his dream. As I talked with this man, Hugh McLean, he shared with me how others had laughed at him when he did his first feature length film. His testimony encouraged me. Remember, God will send others who have gone before you to encourage you.

What was so amazing about this encounter with Hugh McLean was that he started telling me about this major project he was working on at the time and also about the next one he had coming up in a few months. The producer on both of these projects was one of the first Christian producers in the filmmaking industry. As we continued to talk, I also found out that Hugh had met Ron Kenoly years ago and had a strong relationship with him. The Lord was not only setting up these divine connections for me, but He was bringing people to me who already knew each other—people with the same focus and the same heart.

God was revealing His purpose to me one divine connection at a time. For example, I met a football coach named Bobby Bentley who had five state championships under his belt. He spoke about how God had put His hand on his life with divine connections. God formed these relationships for His purpose. His advice to me was to watch as this chain of events unfolded—and if God said to do it, then just do it and don't worry about who will come.

KINGDOM DREAMS KEY POINTS

- ➤ What seems impossible for man is possible with God.

- ➤ Even when we cannot see it, God has a specific plan for success.

- ➤ If God is the initiator of your dream, He is also the provision for it.

- ➤ God will send others who have gone before you to encourage you.

- ➤ If God says do it, just do it and don't worry about who will come.

Chapter 9

~

A Word on Divine
Interventions

by Shekhar Kallianpur

INTRODUCING SHEKHAR KALLIANPUR

When I began talking about kingdom dreams and destiny, I never thought it would consist of producing Christian films. I felt totally unqualified to pursue this dream until God sent me a man from the other side of the world with the same dream in his heart. This man was Shekhar Kallianpur from Mumbai, India—the movie industry capital of the world.

As I mentioned earlier, I was introduced to Shekhar by a spiritual mentor named Satish Raiborde. Satish asked me to meet him to discuss my dream. I was very discouraged at the time and was basically focusing on some upcoming mission trips. After I shared my dream with Satish, he said there was a man who had a dream that sounded identical to mine. Satish invited me to attend an informal dinner with him and a few close associates in Columbia, South Carolina.

After we arrived, my wife and I talked to the host couple as the other guests began arriving. When Shekhar first walked through the door, it was as if I had known him all my life. However, I was hesitant to share my dream because of my experience with others who had only tried to discourage me from pursuing it. Even after I was introduced to him, I remained somewhat withdrawn for most of the night.

I realized I was in a place of fear so I began to talk to the Lord in my heart. "Lord, I don't want to have another connection unless it is a divine appointment from you." Shekhar was about 5 feet away from me on his knees, appearing to be in intense prayer about something. Then he stood up, walked over to me, and began to speak things to me that nobody knew but God. Shekhar began to say things that related to what I had just prayed to God about, and for the next 10 to 15 minutes I knew the Holy Spirit was answering my prayers.

From that moment on, I knew God had brought this man to partner with me in this dream. Shekhar had a vision to bring Bollywood and Hollywood together for Christian filmmaking. We spent days in sweet fellowship and strategic planning and confirmed our mission together for the Kingdom of God.

Clinton C. Baker

SHEKHAR KALLIANPUR—MY STORY

I was born and raised in the Hindu faith, which meant if my salvation was not accepted by my creator, I could be reborn up to

144 times as an animal, or a tree, or whatever. By the time I was eight years old, I believe God gave me a hunger to search and seek Him. I would go to the terrace at the top of my building, close my eyes, and imagine God coming down to take me to Heaven. In my dream I was escaping from this reincarnation cycle and getting into Heaven.

As a young man I got lost in the things of the world and was constantly feeling guilty and condemned. I still had a heart for God and a desire to go to Heaven, but I thought that my salvation was based on works. My dad was a Hindu priest and the most pious man I had ever met, so I asked him, "You have been a Hindu and a pious man so what is your hope of salvation in the next life?" I found that he did not have any assurance of salvation, and he was not even sure he would be reborn as a human being. If he didn't stand a chance, then I felt I was nowhere near Heaven. That gave me an even a greater hunger to seek for a savior who would set me free from the power of sin and give me life eternally.

In my desperate search, I became open to the Muslim faith. I began to do yoga and walk after any man or woman I thought was of God. I would bow down to anyone, worship men, go barefoot, and do anything I thought would help set me free from the power of sin. The more I did these things, the guiltier I felt. Even though on the outside I seemed a peaceful man, inside I was so empty and wretched knowing I was living such a hypocritical life.

THE HOLY SPIRIT WAS SEEKING ME AS I SOUGHT THE TRUTH

I realize now that the Holy Spirit was seeking me even as I sought the truth. It was in my teenage years that someone gave me a Bible and told me Jesus was the way, the truth, and the life. In the midst of my idol worship, I began to read the Bible seeking for a savior. Every night I would read the Word religiously until 2 or 3 a.m. Then one fine night the presence of the Holy Spirit came so strongly as I was reading Isaiah:

> Then he takes what's left and makes his god: a carved idol! He falls down in front of it, worshiping and praying to it. "Rescue me!" he says. "You are my god!" Such stupidity and igno-rance! Their eyes are closed, and they cannot see. Their minds are shut, and they cannot think (Isaiah 44:17-18 NLT).

As I read what God said about idols—that they have eyes but cannot see, and they have ears but cannot hear—I was strongly convicted that what I had been doing was wrong. I was now cer-tain that there was Someone up there who knew my heart, knew what was happening, and was speaking into my life. I began to de-vote more and more time to the Scriptures.

Then one night, I read John 3:16 about how God so loved the world that He gave His Son Jesus Christ that whosoever would believe in Him would have eternal life. I had always thought that Jesus came for the Christians, and the Hindu god came for the Hindus, and Muhammad came for Muslims, and that each reli-gion had its own savior. But this verse said that God loved the world so much that He sent His Son (see John 3:16). I suddenly realized that there was only one God and that He was the Creator of everything.

The One who created the sun, the moon, the stars, and the uni-verse loved me so much that He gave me Jesus. That night I was so convinced, I could not believe in anything else. I had found the an-swer. I understood that I could go to Jesus because He died for my sins on the cross at Calvary. Though I was a sinner, if I put my trust in Jesus I would receive my salvation, the forgiveness of sin and life eternal. That night I just knew that Jesus was the way, the truth, and the life. I did not need anyone else or any tangible proof. I just knew in my spirit that I was to praise and worship the Lord Jesus Christ. I dropped to my knees, began singing the Psalms, and just worshipped the Lord as my Savior.

GROWING IN FAITH AND LOVE FOR THE LOCAL PEOPLE

From that moment on, I faithfully but secretly prayed in my room for people who were sick in the hospital—and they would be healed. One time at my cousin's house, I began to pray for someone over dinner. It was at Christmas time and they asked me to pray for the food, but I began to pray for people. As I prayed, the Holy Spirit touched one of the men, and I was able to minister to him right there at the dinner table. God began to use me. I began to have close encounters of the Holy Spirit in measures I had never experienced before.

God brought me to New Life Fellowship Church where I was discipled in the home church movement. Pastor Joseph led this congregation of only 40 people. Each week we had worship, the Word, and then a workshop on witnessing. The workshop was on-the-job training. As a Hindu boy, now a follower of Jesus, I was like Nicodemus. I did not want to show anyone that I had become a Christian. I was very shy concerning my confession of faith, but nevertheless I knew that Jesus was the way, the truth, and the life. So I continued to associate with these Christians, knowing God had brought me to these families to grow in my faith and in my love for the local people.

Eventually I was made a cell leader and began to lead cells, witness, and pray openly for people. I also began to ask God for the right jobs. It was very difficult to find a job where you could work and live your life for the Lord without compromise. I prayed and asked God to give me a breakthrough in this area. By the time I was 33 years old, I had graduated with a degree in economics, and I was earning a five-figure salary, which was considered impossible for the average Indian boy of that age.

By the time I was 36, the call of God began to motivate me and I just knew that marketplace ministry was my call. This was is in 1986 and 1987. I would serve Jesus and Nestle would pay me a salary for doing the work of the Lord. I began to serve and minister to people in the marketplace and began to share the Gospel with all my dealers and company people. That is how God trained me to reach out to businessmen and people in high finance.

I was then able to start a church in the eastern part of Bombay (what is today called Mumbai). I would travel Monday through Friday and then do the ministry on Saturday and Sunday. This continued for seven years. Every Monday through Friday, I would work where the company sent me and then in the evenings and on Saturday and Sunday, I would minister and serve the Lord.

GOD'S VISION, GOD'S PROVISION

Every Sunday, the church would take a second offering, and for seven years we used this money to go out and preach the Gospel among the poorest areas in India. We would preach the Gospel, pray for people, and God would do signs, wonders, and miracles. We saw hundreds of demons cast out and two people raised from the dead.

Then in 1994, the Lord began to speak to my heart that He was going to use me in America and Europe to preach the Gospel. Others confirmed that God was going to use me this way. Both Dr. Billy Graham and Reinhard Bonnke spoke this prophetic word over my life so I took a big step of faith. I was doing business with an American company, which helped me to travel to many nations as a businessman and to increase my influence all over the world.

Then the business began to decrease and by 1999, my income was zero. I asked the Lord to show me what I was doing wrong. He said, "Son, I am raising you up to apostolically minister to the businessmen of the world." We began to call them the people of the AIR—meaning people of authority, influence, and resources. It meant that we were called to connect with businessmen as well as politicians and people in media. God gave me this strategy to reach one million people in India and beyond. I used to work very hard trying to reach out to large groups of factory workers, but now our strategy was to reach out to the factory owner. When you reach the factory owner, you have the people, the money, the resources, and influence in that city.

Then God had us expand into media. Movies and television were so big and the stars so popular that through them we could reach millions of people. If even one of them came to know the Lord, we could reach out to so many more using God's strategy. I would prophetically tell people that we would be making movies and television programs that would bring the Gospel to people all over the world.

I also declared we would have Hollywood and Bollywood come together. As we do this, I prophesied, we will have churches all over the world that will bring media people and public personalities together to make very big movie productions, so that the Kingdom of Heaven will advance through them.

NOT EVERYONE RECEIVED ME, BUT GOD SENT ENCOURAGEMENT

God sent a powerful evangelist to prophesy over me. This man is so prophetically sharp that he prophesied a year before the elections that the next president of the United States would be a Christian. This was before President George W. Bush Jr. was elected the first time. This man came and spoke this word over me, "Shekhar, you have found something new that will start in this city, and you will have a national and international impact."

I earnestly sought the Lord for about a year, and then God gave us clear direction. "Son, start a prayer meeting, a fellowship that is interdenominational and has all the churches coming together to reach out to businessman, to politicians and bureaucrats, to Bollywood actors and producers. Bring them all together."

It began with just seven people. Today both the Saturday and Sunday meetings minister to more than 800 people. Most of them are very influential. In fact, most of the businessmen are multimillionaires. We have producers, directors, actors, music and sound directors, cameramen, extras, stuntmen, and various technical people all coming together to worship God. They are all saved; they all love Jesus and desire to serve Him. They all say Shekhar is their pastor. By the year 2000, we had more than 40 churches and more than 1,500 people that were under our leadership.

THE BOMBAY CRUSADE

One day some of these multimillionaire businessmen came to me and asked if I thought we could bring Pastor Benny Hinn to India. Four businessmen and I went to Orange County, California, to meet with Pastor Benny Hinn. At first, I do not think he was very impressed with our small group, but I told him these men were very influential. Then I said, "If you will come, it will be one of the largest and the best crusades you ever had in your lifetime."

I do not think he believed what I told him, but after we held the Bombay crusade Pastor Benny Hinn said to me, "Shekhar, this is one of the best crusades I have ever had." There were more than a million people at the crusade, and things went very smoothly—there were no accidents, traffic moved perfectly, the ambience and the presence of God was powerful, and the anointing flowed. Pastor Benny agreed to meet with the businessmen and other community members. This raised up a new standard in the movement in India, where businessman received the anointing of marketplace ministry and began to advance the Kingdom of God in the business world.

A POWERFUL NEW MOVE OF GOD

This began a great new move of God in India. God gave us opportunities to minister to more and more leadership throughout our country. I made it my business to focus on the Word and prayer, and to lead the way for this new move of God that was soon to expand all over the world. My next stop was the United States of America.

As I prepared for a crusade in a church in Lexington, South Carolina, I told God that I wanted to meet with anyone He had for me who would be part of this kingdom harvest. I had received several invitations to speak while I was in America, but I had said no to all of them. As I traveled, my cry and prayer to the Lord was that I wanted to meet those people who had the anointing and the call of God for the end-time harvest. God answered my prayer.

CONNECTING WITH DR. CLINTON BAKER

No matter where I went, I would pray and ask the Holy Spirit to lead me to divine connections. As I traveled, I met more and more people God had in place for this powerful new movement. Then I met Dr. Clinton Baker. One of the first things I said to him was, "Sir, God sent me to tell you, your old season is over and your new season is coming." As we talked, we found God was confirming through me words that had been spoken over him. He talked about the dreams that were in his heart. I believe that God really connected us in a relationship where we were not only free to share our dreams but could also work together to see them come to pass.

KINGDOM DREAMS KEY POINTS

- ➤ Kingdom dreams are not given based on background or qualifications.

- ➤ God will bring diverse people together and bring unity through a kingdom dream.

- ➤ The Holy Spirit needs our cooperation in order to see our dreams materialize.

- ➤ The presence of God is the only atmosphere that will nurture, develop, and birth a kingdom dream.

- ➤ Idols have to be destroyed in our lives before God will manifest His kingdom dream.

- ➤ Jesus Christ must be Lord over our lives and dreams to prevent our dreams from becoming idols in our hearts.

- ➤ Kingdom dreams lead to building up the Kingdom of God.

- ➤ Dreams grow as we grow in relationship with God.

- ➤ God will finance what He conceives.

Chapter 10

Manifesting Your
Kingdom Dream

WHEN IT IS YOUR TIME

From the earliest days of childhood these words would ring in my mind and heart, "When it is your time, nobody can stop what God has ordained for your life." I remember questioning the truth of this statement when it seemed everyone around me was living out their dreams but me. One day my mother sat me down and explained to me that sometimes God will wait until He knows we are mature enough to handle what He is trying to give us. She stressed the importance of patience but I wasn't receiving it. I felt I was ready and God needed to hurry up and make my dream come true.

My mother had a God-given ability to ask questions that would help me see reality. "Do you think you are ready to take on all the responsibility that comes with this dream? Do you think you are ready for people who won't like you or are jealous of you?"

As I tried to answer her heart-probing questions, I knew I was not ready to truly walk in the dream God had ordained for my life.

One of the things we often fail to do is to adequately review our dreams and count the cost to see if we can pay the price to turn our dreams into reality. Jesus asks this same probing question in Luke, "For which of you, intending to build a tower, sitteth not down first, and counteth the cost, whether he have sufficient to finish it?" (Luke 14:28).

We also need to make sure we are in God's perfect timing. Timing is critical in everything we do in life. If we do things too early or too late, we cannot accomplish the purposes of God. For example, Moses was called by God from birth to deliver the Israelites from slavery. The desire to be a deliverer was already within Moses, but he could not function in that calling without proper training. In Exodus chapter 2, we see what can happen when we try to fulfill a purpose out of God's perfect timing:

> And it came to pass in those days, when Moses was grown, that he went out unto his brethren, and looked on their burdens: and he spied an Egyptian smiting a Hebrew, one of his brethren. And he looked this way and that way, and when he saw that there was no man, he slew the Egyptian, and hid him in the sand. And when he went out the second day, behold, two men of the Hebrews strove together: and he said to him that did the wrong, Wherefore smitest thou thy fellow? And he said, Who made thee a prince and a judge over us? Intendest thou to kill me, as thou killedst the Egyptian? And Moses feared, and said, Surely this thing is known. Now when Pharoah heard this thing, he sought to slay Moses. But Moses fled from the face of Pharoah, and dwelt in the land of Midian: and he sat down by a well (Exodus 2:11-15).

As you can clearly see, Moses was out of sync with God's timing. Did God abandon Moses or the dream because Moses missed His timing? Of course not, rather God placed Moses into a dream development training program that lasted for 40 years. God develops the dreamer to fulfill the dream. Isaiah declares that whatever God ordains will happen in His timing, not man's timing. "The Lord of hosts hath sworn, saying, Surely as I have thought, so shall it come to pass; and as I have purposed, so shall it stand" (Isa. 14:24). God has ordained times and seasons for everything and whenever we try to do things either too early or too late, we cause ourselves problems.

We saw what happened when a man tried to fulfill a dream too early, now let's take a look at a king who tries to fulfill an assignment too late. This example involves King Saul and is recorded for us in First Samuel chapter 15. You need to read the entire chapter for the complete details of this story, but for the sake of illustrating this principle, we will examine verses 13-23:

And Samuel came to Saul: and Saul said unto him, Blessed be thou of the Lord: I have performed the commandment of the Lord. And Samuel said, what meaneth then this bleating of the sheep in mine ears, and the lowing of the oxen which I hear? And Saul said, They have brought them from the Amalekites: for the people spared the best of the sheep and of the oxen, to sacrifice unto the Lord thy God; and the rest we have utterly destroyed. Then Samuel said unto Saul, Stay, and I will tell thee what the Lord hath said to me this night. And he said unto him, Say on. And Samuel said, When thou was little in thine own sight, wast thou not made the head of the tribes of Israel, and the Lord anointed thee king over Israel? And the Lord sent thee on a journey, and said, go and utterly destroy the sinners the Amalekites, and fight against them until they be consumed. Wherefore then didst thou not obey the voice of the Lord, but didst fly upon the spoil, and didst evil in the sight of the Lord? And Saul said unto Samuel, Yea, I have obeyed the voice of the Lord, and have gone the way which the Lord sent me, and have brought Agag the king of Amalek, and have utterly destroyed the Amalekites. But the people took of the spoil, sheep and oxen, the chief of things which should have been utterly destroyed, to sacrifice unto the Lord thy God in Gilgal. And Samuel said, Hath the Lord as great delight in burnt offerings and sacrifices, as in obeying the voice of the Lord? Behold, to obey is better than sacrifice, and to hearken than the fat of rams. For rebellion is as the sin of witchcraft, and stubbornness is as iniquity and idolatry. Because thou hast rejected the word of the Lord, He hath also rejected thee from being king (1 Samuel 15:13-23).

This king lost his anointing to be king because he thought he could fulfill God's dream or assignment when and how he chose. There is a danger in not understanding the importance of the time frame assigned by God for a dream. God has a perfect timing that cannot be too early or too late. God will prepare us for our assignment, but we have to remain sensitive to the voice of God to turn the dream into reality. One of the things that will cause us to miss the timing of God is becoming self-focused. We have to tune in to our Lord and Savior Jesus Christ by spending adequate time with Him daily. We will not become sensitive to changes or timing without remaining sensitive to His presence.

We have to love the presence of God more than anything else in life in order to fulfill the will of God and turn our dreams into reality. The presence of God will impregnate, grow, and bring into existence the dream originated from the mind of God. The dream that God has ordained is like a baby that has a delivery date. When it is time for this baby to be born, the natural processes inside the mother's womb will work to bring this seed into manifestation. Heaven and earth will pass away, but God's dream that has been declared in your life must come into existence and be manifested in your life—in His timing.

MANIFESTATION

Over the years the Spirit of God has impacted my heart with the word *manifestation*. I once heard an apostle give a powerful teaching on the word *manifest*, and I want to share with you what I learned. According to the *American College Dictionary*, the word *mani*, from which we get the English word *manual*, means "of or pertaining to the hand." The word *festa*, from which we get the word *festival*, means "advancing or celebrating." Basically when we put the two words together, we get "advancing the hand of God."

So when you see *manifest* in Scripture it means "the hand of God is upon that person." The Holy Spirit will manifest Himself in man through the gifts of the Spirit. First Corinthians reads, "But the manifestation of the Spirit is given to each one for the profit of all" (1 Cor. 12:7 NKJV). God's Spirit physically uses His people to reveal or advance His purposes in us for the profit of all.

God's hand must be upon a person for the dream to manifest. When it comes to a kingdom dream, God's hand has to be upon a person. It cannot be just what one thinks or wants. It has to be the Holy Spirit causing a person to become pregnant with this dream. It is no different than how after a child is conceived it must go through a developing process over the next nine months. As you go through the development stages for your kingdom dream, there is a day and a time set for that dream's birth. The enemy will attempt to kill the dream before its due date through spiritual warfare.

Spiritual Warfare

In mentioning spiritual warfare, here I am talking about the warfare that we go through where the enemy tries to make us quit before the dream can ever be born. There is a specific time I remember when I was staying in an apartment in London, and I was experiencing all kinds of attacks upon my body and in my mind. I had tried to share my pain with others, but I just could not seem to make anybody understand what I was experiencing. Many would tell me I just needed to have more faith. I was discouraged, hurting, and I felt like quitting.

Not that I had not experienced spiritual warfare before, but I had never experienced it to this level or intensity. Day in and day out, from the time I woke up and then all throughout the day, I was fighting intense physical and mental attacks. When I would go to sleep, I would wake up in the middle of the night to fight some more. I was not getting much sleep so I was extremely tired. I know now that this is the type of warfare that happens right before God manifests something powerful in my life. But at that time what I needed was someone to say to me, "Hey man, I understand what you are going through, and I am here to encourage you."

All I could think about were the many prophetic words that had been spoken over me, and how I was supposed to be this powerful international minister. How could I quit? I tried reminding myself of all the people who wanted to become part of this dream. But it always came back to what I was dealing with physically and emotionally at the moment.

I turned the television to TBN London, and Dr. Zachery Tims was preaching. He said, "Some of you just got knocked down, and you feel like giving up and quitting." I said to myself this has got to be a word from God. He went on to say, "Right before God manifested some things in my life and my ministry, all hell broke out against my mind and my body." I prayed, "Thank you Lord, for sending a man of God who has already gone through what I am experiencing."

God also used another man to minister to me so I would not quit. Ronald Raiborde had been in London over thirty years. He knew all about the warfare I had been experiencing. It was like he had read my mail. I had been praying for the Lord to expand my territory. God answered my prayer but I found I could not seem to handle the intense fighting needed to move into this expansion. Ronald Raiborde looked straight at me and said, "Now go to all the world. Don't quit. The enemy wants you to quit."

As I was listening to him, I remembered how many times I had heard people prophesy to me saying I was to go to the nations. I had been pleading with God to help me get stronger so I could go and do what He wanted me to do. Then I realized He had brought deliverance into my life through others who had faced what I was facing. He had me deal with old childhood feelings of rejection and fear. I began to understand that God's plan is multifaceted in the midst of manifesting a kingdom dream.

As I continued to listen to this man's testimony, God brought me to that peace only He can give. I suddenly realized I could get through this even though I did not know every step to take. I clearly saw that God was using others to encourage me all along the way. I knew the path still might not be easy, but I could rest in the calm assurance that God is with me, watching over me every step of the way.

The Flesh Must Die So the Dream Can Manifest

Three powerful truths now permeated my thoughts:

- We never get deliverance by keeping our dreams from manifesting.

- No one can fully manifest kingdom dreams through manipulation.

- Flesh cannot handle it, so flesh has to totally die in order for the dream to manifest.

I realized I was experiencing a crushing in areas of my life that would stand in the way of the full manifestation of the dream. There are things God is still trying to remove in my life, but I know He will never send me more than I can handle at any given time. My desire now is to cooperate with the work of the Holy Spirit in me and make sure that I let God take everything out of me which could give the enemy a foothold—such as fears, insecurities, or lack of confidence.

The kingdom dream is so important to God that the enemy will try anything to kill it. When he sends in his big guns, that is when I know I have got to keep moving forward. That is the moment of truth, the danger point, the fork in the road. That is where I must choose to believe what God says or be swayed by the circumstances all around me. I must not only say that I am in Christ, but I have got to live my life and literally be in Christ. My character, my life, and everything I do must reveal the Christ in me. My life must exemplify the verse, "Greater is He that is in you, than he that is in the world" (1 John 4:4).

KINGDOM DREAMS KEY POINTS

- The dream that God has ordained is like a baby with a delivery date.

- God's hand must be upon a person for the dream to manifest.

- God's plan is multifaceted in the midst of manifesting a kingdom dream.

- We never get deliverance by keeping our dreams from manifesting.

- No one can fully manifest kingdom dreams through manipulation.

- Flesh cannot handle it, so flesh has to totally die in order for the dream to manifest.

- My life must exemplify, "Greater is He that is in you, than he that is in the world" (1 John 4:4).

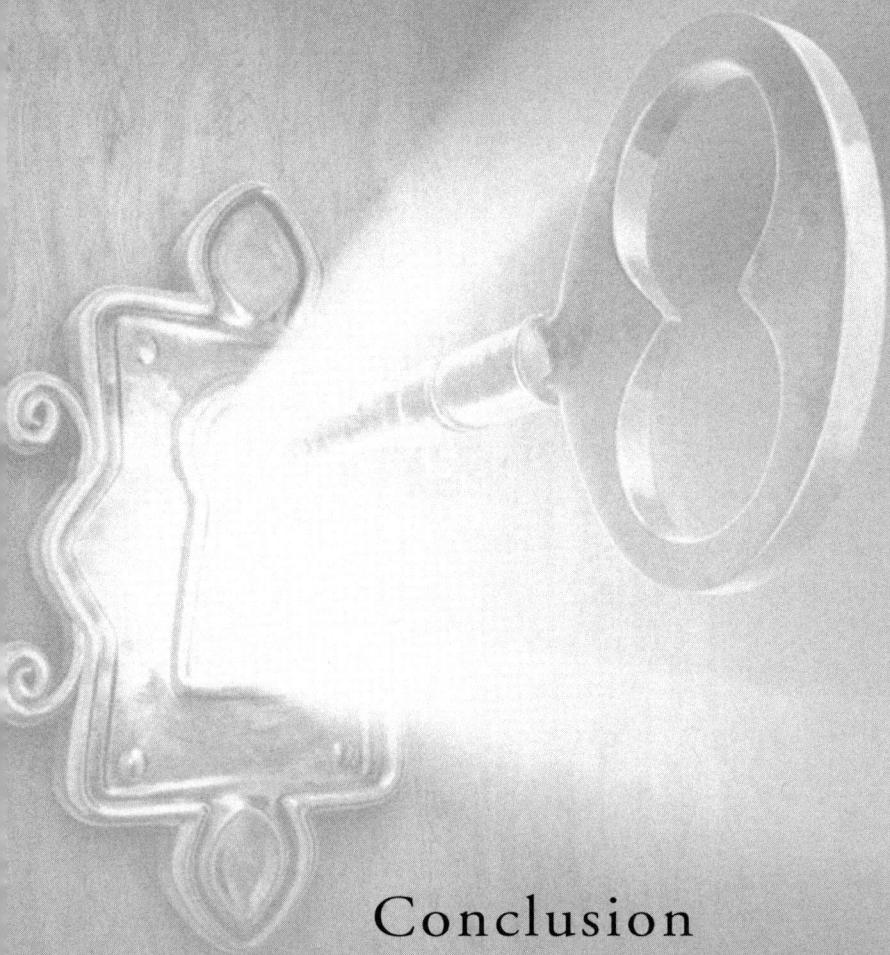

Conclusion

DREAM
KINGDOM DREAMS!

There is one more divine connection I must mention here before we conclude this book. In working out the details of Ron Kenoly coming to my "Kingdom Dream" conference, I formed a relationship with his secretary. One day as I was talking with her she said, "There is somebody else you need to meet. His name is Dr. Larry Keefauver. He is a prolific writer, and you two need to talk. Larry and his wife Judi just left here. He had on one of your kingdom dream t-shirts, and it made me think of you. I am going to give you his cell number. Call him." As I agreed to make the call I was thinking to myself, *Who is Dr. Larry Keefauver?*

I really did not think anymore about it as I prepared for the upcoming Sunday service. I drove to church and, as usual, I had my Smith Wigglesworth books in my car. I preached, came home, and was relaxing in my study when the Holy Spirit said, "Go to your bag and look at your books." I have learned to be obedient to the promptings of the Holy Spirit, so I took my books out of the bag. The Holy Spirit asked me, "Who wrote these books?" I looked at the author page and it said, Dr. Larry Keefauver. The Lord reminded me that years ago I had said I wanted to thank the author and tell him what a blessing these devotionals had been to me.

These Smith Wigglesworth devotionals had fueled my faith when I was dealing with times of discouragement and fighting off panic attacks. I have had these books for years and still read them for strength and encouragement. One time as I was reading them, I asked God to let me connect with the man who wrote these books so I could thank him for making these materials available. Through a divine connection, we met and this book is a result of our meeting.

I thank God for each and every one of the many divine connections He has already given me, and for those that are yet to come as I continue to pursue the kingdom dream He has placed in my heart.

A Word From Dr. Larry Keefauver

A kingdom dream comes from God. Joseph declared that only God could interpret dreams. Now that Clinton Baker has so eloquently described this process and imparted it to you through this powerful book, you must act on what you have received.

Abide. Now is the time for you to abide in God's presence so that His presence may birth His dreams in you. Remember, with God all things are possible. When you dream His impossible dreams, those dreams become possible because of their Source— the living God.

Hear God's voice. Do not chase a rabbit trail interpretation concerning what you think a dream means. Instead, let God interpret the dream for you. Listen to His voice; trust His word; then obey.

Faithfully obey God. Dreams become reality only when we trust and obey. Joseph not only received dreams from God. He declared by faith what they revealed and walked in obedience to God's commands.

Are you ready to receive, understand, and then act upon God's kingdom dreams in your life? If so, dream on—empowered by the living God!

FINAL NOTE—THE LORDSHIP OF JESUS CHRIST

God will not work for us when we are working against His Word or His way of doing things. God holds our dreams in His hands, but we must recognize that He has the power to perform, delay, or even deny them. When we come under the lordship of Jesus Christ, God will personally open doors for us and close other doors that need to be closed. Revelation explains:

> *And to the angel of the church in Philadelphia write; These things saith He that is holy, He that is true, He that hath the key of David, He that openeth, and no man shutteth; and shutteth, and no man openeth (Revelation 3:7).*

The dream that fulfills our destiny belongs to God. We are only stewards of what God has given us. Whenever we view our dreams and destiny, we should remember that Jesus is Lord. Whenever we start to take lordship over our lives and dreams, we lose divine assistance and enablement. Whenever we cease to make His lordship evident in our lives, we will notice doors shutting until there is a genuine repentance. There is great danger in putting ourselves in the place that belongs to God.

Romans chapter 1 contains a warning that we must not take lightly:

> *For the wrath of God is revealed from heaven against all ungodliness and unrighteousness of men, who hold the truth in unrighteousness; because that which may be known of God is manifest in them; for God hath shewed it unto them. For the invisible things of Him from the creation of the world are clearly seen, being understood by the things that are made, even His eternal power and Godhead; so that they are without excuse: because that, when they knew God, they glorified Him not as God, neither were thankful; but became vain in their imaginations, and their foolish heart was darkened. Professing themselves to be wise, they became fools, and changed the glory of the uncorruptible God into an image made like to corruptible man, and to birds, and fourfooted beasts, and creeping things. Wherefore God also gave them up to uncleanness through the lusts of their own hearts, to dishonour their own bodies between themselves: who changed the truth of God into a lie, and worshipped and served the creature more than the Creator, who is blessed for ever. Amen* (Romans 1:18-25).

If you do not have a personal relationship with Jesus Christ or have not allowed Him to be Lord of your life, I encourage you to pray this prayer:

> *Lord Jesus, I accept You as Lord, ruler, and controller of my life and destiny. I ask You to work in my life from this day forward, to help me to turn every dream that You have placed in my heart into reality. By your grace. Amen.*

If you prayed this prayer, please contact me at www.valiantministries.net and let me know so we can add you to our INCF prayer list for dreams to be turned into reality.

CONTACT THE AUTHOR

If you would like to contact the author,
please visit the website at:

www.valiantministries.net

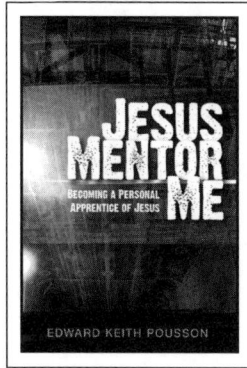

Additional copies of this book and other book
titles from DESTINY IMAGE™ EUROPE
are available at your local bookstore.

We are adding new titles every month!

To view our complete catalog online, visit us at:
www.eurodestinyimage.com

Send a request for a catalog to:

D★ Destiny Image™ Europe

Via Acquacorrente, 6
65123 - Pescara - ITALY
Tel. +39 085 4716623 - Fax +39 085 9431270

"Changing the world, one book at a time."

Are you an author?

Do you have a today, God-given message?

CONTACT US

We will be happy to review your
manuscript for the possibility of publication:

publisher@eurodestinyimage.com
http://www.eurodestinyimage.com/pages/AuthorsAppForm.htm